LEAHY LAND DEED NOTES
1708-1950

DAVID LEAHY

Issue 2

ISBN:
ISBN-13: 978-0995663015
ISBN-10: 0995663017

1   Introduction

What follows is a table containing notes on deeds of the Lahy / Lahey / Leahy / Lahee surnames (as seller) from the years 1708 – 1950.

Not everyone can afford to visit Ireland and access the Registry of Deeds or other libraries and spend the amount of time required to look up indexes, and then find the relevant Deed in the huge heavy Deeds books (see Figure 1). Then to find individual deeds and read through the difficult to interpret legal language present in the deeds - and believe me it takes a long time - as well as muscle - the books quite often weigh 10Kg or more!

Figure 1 Registry of Deeds - Henrietta Street Dublin

After a few weeks I became adept at speed reading the deeds and extracting the relevant people, lands and relationships (if present) within the text of the deed. I recorded every Leahy / Lahy / Lahey / Lahee name present in the Lessee indexes. I made notes on all of the Cavan based Leahys but also recorded the other Leahys seller and buyer names and deed number from all over Ireland. Thus, the reader can send for the full deed if either the summary provided or the recorded seller / buyer names is of interest.

I spent many days in the Registry of Deeds in Henrietta Street Dublin lifting the very heavy large books and systematically going through all of the Indexes and recording the presence of Lahy / Leahy / Lahee sellers of land (Note: some of the deeds are Wills and some are Marriage articles.

Mostly I've recorded the key people dates and land details that I could decipher. In some instances, I have transcribed the whole deeds which are available in section 4.

Most deeds are from the Registry of Deeds. A few are located in the National Library of Ireland (Kildare Street, Dublin).

Further information on the early Leahy families in county Cavan is available in:

Ref 1 - *The Cavan Leahys: Origins*. – D. G. Leahy
Ref 2 – *The Cavan Leahys: 1800-1950* – D. G. Leahy
Ref 3 - *The Laheys: Pioneer Settlers and Sawmillers*. – S. Lahey

Should the reader wish to view the original deed from the Registry of Deeds – address at end of this book and send it off to The Registry of Deeds in Dublin and they will send you the original deed – Fee €20 [as of 2018].

Note that other Deeds exist in some private collections and there are also notes on Wills made e.g. by Betham that exist in the Betham Will abstracts. These are analysed in Ref 1 and some are transcribed in section 5 . In addition, Wills (post 1858) exist in the National Archives in Dublin.

Registry of Deeds Look Up Procedure

In the Registry of Deeds, one can either look up deeds by 'Seller' name or by Townland. To look up the seller, you must choose the decade you're interested in, then retrieve the appropriate Seller Index. In the seller Index most of the names are arranged alphabetically. Thus, one can quickly look up the 'Leahy' / 'Lahy' surnames etc and note down the book Number, page number and Memorial Number. One then goes to the Memorial room to retrieve that particular book, page and memorial (Deed). Then you have to try and read and interpret the sometimes difficult to comprehend 'legal language' of the day.

Buyers

Unfortunately, there are no indexes of 'Buyers'. to identify Leahy 'buyers' one would have to mandraulically go through every single Index of every surname in the Registry of deeds 'Seller' Index and search for 'Leahys' as the 'buyer. Although I did this for a few (and they're recorded at the end.), I didn't have the time or patience to do this, but perhaps someone in future may devise a way to perform this task efficiently.

Note that the either the Property Registration Authority or the National Library of Ireland retains the copyright in relation to the original deeds.

If the reader believes they are related to the 'Cavan' branch of the Leahy / Lahy / Lahey clan then please get in touch as I'm continually trying to add connections to the Leahy family tree I am building and may have information on your ancestors. Email address is cavanleahys@gmail.com. There is also a *Facebook* group you are welcome to join to participate in live discussions and post your own stories / photos – 'Cavan Leahys'.

2 Seller / Lessor Deeds Notes

Note that Deeds with 'Full Trans' listed in the Date Column have been fully transcribed and are available in Appendix A.

.

1708-1730

From	To	Book No	Page No	Memorial No	Notes	
Lahy	Lahy	82	458	58573	John lahy of aghakilmore to William (his son) and to Mary his daughter and wife of William Heeny (son in law) – lands of lower aghakilmore. Witnessed by Thomas Heany of upper castletown Westmeath, and John Lahy of Upper Aghakilmore, Hugh Flanagan of Mill Castle Westmeath and Reilly of Dublin	1719 (Reg 1736) Full Trans

1730-1745

From	To	Book No	Page No	Memorial No	Notes	
Edmund Lahy	Welsh	112	224	77775	Edmund Lahey of Pennane, Tipperary to Patrick Welsh	1730
Edmund Lahy		119	13	80399	Edmund Lahey of Pennane, Tipperary	
Dillon Collard	Sizers			63769	FULL TRANS	1730
Lahy	Downes	80	217	55583	John, Henry & Thomas of Upper Aghakilmore sold to Rev Dive Downes 50 acres in upper Aghakilmore and 11 acres in Lavagh (3/4 of the estate of Thomas Lahy (deceased)	1735 Full Trans
Fitzpatrick	Lahy			57842	Richard Fitzpatrick of Aghakilmore in the county of Cavan, gentleman and Fitzpatrick of Derrin in the said county son of Richard of the one part and Henry	1735

					Lahy of Upper Aghakilmore lands of Middle Aghakilmore witnessed by William Lahy, Oliver Cheevers, John Lahy and Thomas Lahy	
Lahy	Downes	88	470	63321	John Lahy of Lower Aghakilmore to Rev Dive Downes of Castlecourt in Meath 70 Acres in lower Aghakilmore, part of the estate of Richard Lahy (deceased) father of John Lahy. Witnessed by Edward Fitzgerald of Moate and Francis Freeman of Castlecor and William Rain (Servant of Dive Downes) and Edward Sterling of Dublin	1738
John Lahy	Lahy	95	248	66369	John Lahy of Lower Aghakilmore and William Lahy of Up Aghakilmore. 35 Acres in lower aghakilmore. Witnessed by William Blakely of Aughafad, Jam(es) Lahy and John Lahy of Upper Aghakilmore & Bxxx Delaney (Dublin Gent). 19 Acres in Lavagh and Aghacreevy.	1738
Pritchard	Haughton			63539	FULL TRANS	1738
Arthur Lahy	Downes	94	304	66435	Arthur and Francis Lahy both of Moate moyaresten, Cavan, to Rev Dive Downes of castlecor, Meath 66 Acres in Moate, mayabrasten, clonmahon formerly the estate of Richard Lahy of Aghakilmore (deceased) Witnessed by Edward Fitzgerald of Moate.	1739

					Thomas Lahee, and Edward Sterling of Dublin	
John Lahy	Lahy	95	249	66370	John Lahy of Lower Aghakilmore and Francis Lahy (nephew) of Upper Moydristan in county Afones. 66 Acres in Upper Moydristan in Parish of Ballymachugh. Witnessed by William Lahy of Lower Aghakilmore, Thomas Lahy and John Lahy of Upper Aghakilmore	1739
John Lahy	Lahy	95	249	66371	John Lahy of Lower Aghakilmore and Henry Lahy of Upper Aghakilmore (nephew). 35 Acres in lower Aghakilmore and 19 Acres of Lavagh and Aghacreevy. Witnessed by William Blakely of Aughafad and James and John Lahy of Upper Aghakilmore.	1739

1746-1757

From	To	Book No	Page No	Memorial No	Notes	
Leahy	O'Brien	142	552	98326		
Leahy	Daunt	154	277	103670		
Leahy	Hammon	150	534	103743		
Lacky	Kearney	162	29	108211		

1758-1768

From	To	Book No	Page No	Memorial No	Notes	
John Lahy	Lahy	202	591	135902	John Lahy of Tycullen & Henry Lahy of Aughakilmore Lower (1760). Henry paid £60 for 70 Acres in Lower Aughakilmore. Witnessed	1760

John Lahy	Lahy	202	591	135904	by James McClean Innkeeper of Aughakilmore Middle, Henry Strong farmer and James Killroy, Schoolmaster and Thomas Lahy of Aughakilmore Lower. William Lahy of Tycullen transferred unto John Lahy of Lower Aghakilmore half his right of lands in Lavagh being one forth part of the said premises with the appurtenaces for 21 years from 1st day of 1762 at the yearly rent of 9 schillings. The said John under penalty of £20 would not demise said property payable unto the said William. 7/6/1760 Witnessed by Thomas Lahy of Aughakilmore and James Kilroy of Tawlaught. Witnessed by Thomas Lahy and Stephen Rice of Dublin. (William & John brothers ?)	1760
Thomas Lahy(Elder)	Reilly	218	300	143581	Thomas Lahy (Elder) of Aughkilmore that part adjoining David Kellets land and Killykan. 37 Acres 3 roads of lower Aughakilmore to the lands of Aughakilmore bog, in all 40 Acres. For 22 years at yearly rent of 10 pounds and 10 schillings. Witnessed by Cahaire	1761

					Reilly of Killydream and Thomas Lahy (Jun) of Aughakilmore	
William Lahy	Cheevers	217	280	143827	William Lahy of Lavagh to Thomas Cheevers and Thomas Heaney both of Aghakilmore half of all his lands in Lavagh being the one forth part of the said premises to hold during the term of 21 years from 1s May next – yearly rent 15 s per acre. Witnessed by Richard Cheevers of Lis Nugent & Oliver Cheevers his son & Hugh Reilly of Finea (Yeoman) and Robert Acheson of Dublin	1762
Thomas Lahy	Cheevers	217	280	143828	Thomas Lahy of Lower Aghakilmore sold to Thomas Cheevers of Upper Aghakilmore half of Upper Aghakilmore for the term of 21 years. Lease commencing 1st May 1763 at yearly rent of £14 5s 6d. Witnessed by Richard Cheevers of Lis Nugent & Oliver Cheevers his son & William Lahy and Henry Lahy of Lower Aghakilmore.	1762
William Lahy	Lahy	220	531	146370	William Lahy of Tycullen and John Lahy of Aughakilmore – William released and granted onto said John all part of the town and lands of Aughakilmore whereon the John then Lived & agreed for fee £5 Sterling. Witnessed by Thomas Lahy, Henry Lahy, James Lahy and James Kilroy all of Aughakilmore.	1763

					Henry & Thomas Smyth & William MaGrath of Dublin 21/3/1763	
William Lahy	Acheson / Cheevers	229	87	149470	William Lahy of Lavagh sell onto Thomas Cheevers of Aughakilmore all that half of the said William Lahys undivided moiety or half part of the lands of Lavagh and Aghacreevy now in the possession of the said William, Lahy, Thomas Lahy and James Lahy as the same is now held by the said Thomas Cheevers the said part undivided thereby demised to the said Thomas Cheevers containing 16 acres to hold for 30 years. Witnessed Robert Cordner, Robert Acheson	1764
William Lahy	Lahy	248	513	160734	16/4/1766. William Lahy of Lavagh £240 paid by James Lahy of Aughakilmore upper lands of Lavagh and Aghacreevy. Witnessed by Thomas Lahy of Aghakilmore Lower...	1766
Joseph Lahy & Wife	Bell	249	553	166410	Joseph and Mary Lahy (Wife) of Kilnaleck to Andrew Bell of Bellsgrove, 76 Acres in Lower Aghakilmore, witnessed by John Castles of Cavan Town and Patrick Tarvelly of Crossdoney	1767
James Lahy	Lear	264	166	167490	James and Joseph Lahy (Brothers) of Carlow and Hugh Carr (linen weaver) – Lands in Carlow	1767

1768-1776						
From	**To**	**Book No**	**Page No**	**Memorial No**	**Notes**	
John Lahy & Wife	Brady & Wife	260	479	174157	William Lahy of Lavagh and Pat Brady of Dublin and John Lahy of Lower Aghakilmore and his mother Susanne Lahy. 35 Acres in Lower Aghakilmore witnessed by Francis David and William McGrath	1767-1769 Full Trans
William Lahy	Lahy	273	349	177801	1769. William Lahy of Lavagh. £240 paid by James Lahy of Aughakilmore Upper lands of Lavagh and Aghacreevy. Witnessed by Thomas Lahy of Aughakilmore Lower	1769
Joseph Lahy	Lahy	279	494	183906	Joseph Lahy of Kilnaleck [*Check Joseph Will??]* and Henry Lahy of Aughakilmore . Joseph Lahy in consideration of £120 paid by Henry Lahy all part and lands of Aughakilmore known by name of Lower Aughakilmore, containing 70 Acres to hold forever, subject nevertheless to a provisional condition of redemption of payment of said sum with interest for the same as the rate of £10 per year. Default on payments then it shall be lawful for Henry to foreclose Mortgage executed by John Lahy, late of Aughakilmore aforesaid deceased to the said Henry Lahy for the principal sum of £60 on the said lands of Aughakilmore to sell the said Mortgaged premises in which	1770

					said recorded deeds are contained. As Witnessed by James Lahy of Upper Aughakilmore & Patrick Tarvilly of Crossdoney & William Magrath of Dublin & James Lahy, Patt Harvely & Joseph (his mark x) Lahy	
James Lahy	Crosby	292	555	193216	James Lahy of Carlow	1772
Thomas Lahy	Chievers	281	389	187079	Thomas Lahy of Lower Aghakilmore to Thomas Cheevers of Upper Aghakilmore Lands for 31 years at yearly rent of $14 7s 6d. witnessed by Richard Cheevers, Samuel Cheevers, Thomas McManus & James Sheridan	1771
Thomas Lahy	Cheevers	291	529	192786	Thomas Lahy of Lower Aghakilmore to Thomas Cheevers of Upper Aghakilmore. £225 for 25 Acres.	1772
William Lahy & Wife	Lahy	288	315	190877	1772. William Lahy and Wife Elizabeth of Lavagh. And James Lahy of Mullaghboy	1772
William Lahy	Lahy	290	451	193166	1772. William and Elizabeth and James Lahy of Aughakilmore Upper	1772
William Lahy		297	708	196816	William Lahy of Lavagh and Elizabeth Lahy his wife and James Lahy of Mullaghboy and James Lahy of Ballina. Voluntary settlement, unfair purposes. Witnesses William Cother of Dublin and John Faith of Cortal.	1773
William Lahy		301	652	203250	William Lahy and Elizabeth Lahy his wife of Aughakilmore Upper. James Lahy of Aghakilmore. £148 for land in Lavagh and	1775

					Aghacreevy, now held by Bayan Brady – 8 Acres and 24 Acres purchased by James Lahy from William Lahy. Witnessed by Thomas McManus of Ballykeelin, Henry Lahy of Aghakilmore Lower. Thomas Fitzpatrick of Curivoy, and Francis Lahy of Ballina	
William Lahy	Daly	316	26	209461	William Lahy of William Street, Dublin. Shoemaker.	1776

1777-1785

From	To	Book No	Page No	Memorial No	Notes	
Charles Lahy	Fairborough	317	362	218010	Charles Lahy of London (wig maker) and William fiarborough of Carlow. James Lahy's concerns. Witnessed by James William Lahy.	
Francis Lahy	Burrows	National Library of Ireland			Francis Lahy / Rebecca Burrows Marriage Articles	1779 Full Trans
Francis Lahy	Burrows	333	274	224102	Francis Lahy, eldest son and heir at law of James Lahy of Upper Aghakilmore and Rebecca Burrowes 3rd daughter of Killicuman and John Lahy of Williamstown. Dowry of Rebecca £200 to said James Lahy. Alexander Burrowes and James Lahy did grant 60 acres land	1780

					in Upper Aghakilmore (possessed by James Lahy). Witnessed by Stuart Mulligan of Dublin (Gent), Patrick Reilly of Aghakilmore aforesaid Yeoman and Reverend William Wade of Bromhill and James Fitzsimmons of the city of Dublin. Witnessed 16/6/1780.	
Lahy	Read	358	348	241032		
Lahy	Kierr	366	410	243816		
Henry Lahy	Lahy	327	223	216909	Henry Lahy of Aghakilmore and Henry Lahy his son. One half of the lands of Aghakilmore for 999 years. Yearly rent 5 shillings. Witnessed by John Strong and Robert Strong of Tawlaught and William McGrath of Dublin	1778
John Lahy	Walker	326	82	214253	John Lahy of Caprah and Alex Walker from Williamstown, Westmeath and Dorcas Walker, daughter of the said Alex. Marriage between John and Dorcas Walker to John. Lands of Williamstown formerly in the	1777

					possession of widow Duffy and half of lands in Togher in possession of Alex Walker. The said John Lahy in possession of lands of Moat and Middle Aghakilmore. If Dorcas survives John then she receives the lands in Moat and £25 a year for life. Witnessed by Robert Stratford of Dublin and Joseph Brownes of Finae (Westmeath) and John Lahy of Aghakilmore and Richard Cheevers of Lismach, Westmeath.	
James Lahy	Lee	317	317	217843	James Lahy of Thantley in Co Tipperary to Lee	1778
James Lahy	Sayle	318	405	218382		
James Lahy	Bell	340	511	231422		
James Lahy	O Reilly	358	535	243019		
James Lahy	Kerr	366	410	245816		
James Lahy	Fairlough	368	186	246690		
James Lahy	Bell	340	511	231422	James Lahy of Lavagh and Joseph Lahy of Aghakilmore (Brothers ?) and John Bell from Creevy, Longford. Sold lands in	1780

					Lavagh (in possession of tenants James Smyth and Henry Gallaghan) and lands in Aghakilmore in possession of Patrick and Lawrence Reilly for 31 years £251 9s 2d witnessed by George and Hugh Kerr of Granard (Longford).	
Joseph Lahy	Lahy	338	271	227627	1781 – Joseph Lahy of Aughakilmore and Henry Lahy great second son and heir at law of Henry Lahy late of Aughkilmore. 20/7/1764 - £ 120	1781
Lahy	Lahy	334	61	222029	Thomas Lahy of Lower Aughkilmore & wife Margaret and John Lahy of Williamstown in the county of Westmeath Seized and possessed of an estate of inheritance in the town and lands of Aghakilmore Upper now in the tenure of Thomas Heany and Lower Aghakilmore in the Possession of John Masterson, Henry Lahy and the said Thomas Lahy containing 60 Acres. Thomas	1779 FULL TRANS

					Lahy received 5 shillings from John Lahy. Witnessed by William Lahy of Aughakilmore and George M Farran and Bryan Carry of the city of Dublin.	
Thomas Lahy	Lahee	334	61	9	Thomas Lahy of Lower Aughakilmore and Wife Margaret, and John Lahy of Williamstown. 13/12/1779. Henry Lahy. 60 Acres 5 Schillings. Thomas sold land to John for 5 Schillings. Witnessed by William Lahy.	1779
Thomas Lahy	Booth	325	506	222030	Thomas and Margaret Lahy of Aghakilmore and Elinor Booth otherwise Lahy and John Lahy his son, both of Williamstown. Witnessed by Francis Lahy of Ballina.	1779
Maxwell	Pat Lahy	Farnham Papers – Lease to Patt Lahy 1782 - Aughafad		NLI	Royalties Turf Bogs reserved lives of Patt Lahy Lessee, William Lahy eldest son of John Lahy Lessee and William Lahy eldest son of James Lahy of Mullaghboy. Build within 5 years 45Ft long 16Ft wide and 10Ft high with one Acre for an Orchard. Ren £2	1782

From	To	Book No	Page No	Memorial No	Notes	
					Add Rent not to Alien more than 5 Acres at risk of being dispossessed. Bound to Mills Ren £5 a barrel. Not to commit or suffer to be committed any wante in woods and the power for landlord to examine builings and to keep thereif not rep within 6 months after notice.Ten to have half the trees they plant.	
Thomas Lahy	Hunt	351	451	237230	Thomas Lahy of Cappah, Inn holder. Co. Tipperary to William Hunt. £70 Furniture and cattle. Michael Lahy of Cappah witness	1783
Thomas Lahy	Kennedy	361	283	243839	Peter Cook of Gargney Co Tipperary and Thomas Lahy of Cappah and Owen Lahy his wife.	1784
John Leahy	Folow	392	541	259925	Of Borrado, Cork	
Francis Leahy	Sheridan	286 ?	525	257405		
John Lahy	Freeman Wilton			202256	FULL TRANS	1785

1786-1793

From	To	Book No	Page No	Memorial No	Notes	
Francis Lahy	Maxwell	373	505	249281	Francis Lahy of Ballina and Henry Maxwell. Witnessed by xxx Strong	1785

					of Tawlaught and James Lord of Ballynahxxxx	
Francis Lahy	Bell	377	133	250840	James Lahy and Francis Lahy of Killconnell, Cavan and John Bell of Creevy, Longford. Said Jo Lahy in debit to John Bell by his bond 24/5/1779 for. £567 2s, 8d Debt. And also by his the said James Lahy and Francis Lahy joint bond for £1000. On the 2 bonds there is now due the principal interest and costs the sum of £500 sterling. And in order to pay off the said debt, James and Francis in consideration of 10s each of them shall sold onto John Bell one annuity or yearly bond of forty pounds to be issued out of the town and lands of Lavagh in the possession of the representatives of Thomas Cheevers containing 16 Acres also lands in Lavagh in possession of Geo McFarrens – 8 Acres also lands in Lavagh in possession of James Lahy – 42 Acres. For 41 Years. Witnessed by Andrew Bell city of Dublin Kilconny, (Belturbet, Cavan) Kilconny Part of Urban (Belturbet, Cavan) Killyconnan Cuttragh (Cavan)	1786

James Lahy	Kerr	377	132	250839	James Lahy of Lavagh and Francis Lahy of Killcomell? And George Kerr of Finea in Westmeath, Lands of Lavagh now in the possession of representatives of Thomas Cheevers or their under tenants. 16 Acres and Lavagh lands in the possession of James Lahy or his under tenants. 45 Acres.	1786 Full Trans
Richard Leahy		371	326	249651	Cork & Kinsale	
Maxwell	Pat Lahy			NLI Farnham Papers – Lease to Patt Lahy 1789 - Lavagh	Royalties Turf Bogs reserved. Lives of Patt Lahy lessee, Elizabeth Lahy his wife and Catherine Lahy eldest daughter to lessee two years old. Builds within 24" 35 Ft long 14Ft wide and 8Ft high with half an acre for an orchard. £2 Add rent dictating within 5 years 40 Perches 5Ft deep and 6Ft Wide. Ren £1 add Rent not to Alien more than 2 Acres Ren £3 add Rent bound to Mills Ren 75 a branch not to commit or suffer to be com any wake in woods and Ren £10 for every time starter is so committed. Power for landlord to examine buildings and retain them if not rep within 6 months after notice. Tennant to have half the trees and plants.	1789
William Leahy		409	292	268433		1789
David /		403	498	269948		1789

Daniel Leahy						
John Leahy		414	464	272210		1789
Lahiff		423	4	275478	James and John Lahiff, Milltown, Limerick	1790
Leahy, Edmund	William Leahy	433	424	283808		
Lahy, Patrick	Mahon	459	121	293087	Patrick Lahy of Lornha in Co Tipperary and John Mahon	1792
Lahy, Richard	Thornton	459	342	294154	Richard Lahy of Aughakilmore and Francis Thornton of Larkhill (Meath) and Elizabeth Thornton (Spinster) daughter of Francis. Richard Lahy and Elizabeth to marry. Witnessed by Ralph Thornton.	1792
Leahy Rev John	McFhee	443	543	287153	Rev John Leahy of Freck in City of Dublin and James McFee of Ballyconra in Co Kilkenny	1791
Leahy, John	Turner	474	440	302135		
Leahy, William	Jolly	447	481	290680	William Leahy of College Green, Dublin	1792
Lahy, Thomas	John	461	514	296468	Thomas and John Lahy of Lower Aghakilmore and Thomas Arkins of Killgolough, Cavan and Jane Arkins (daughter).£150 for lands in upper and lower Aughakilmore. Witnessed by John Lahy of Williamstown, Westmeath, Thomas Strong of Tawlaught and James w. Devall of Killgolough. *Long deed.*	1790
Lahy, Francis	Burrows	461	514	299871		1790
Lahy,	Maxwell	479	29	300648	Richard Lahy of	1793

Richard					Aughakilmore and Henry Maxwell of Crover, Cavan £479 for Lands in Aughakilmore known as the 'Crofs'. Witnessed by Robert Coyle (Dublin).	

1794-1799

From	To	Book No	Page No	Memorial No	Notes	
Michael Lahy	Kissane	395	153	261412	Tipperary	
Lahee	Martin	409	371	268619	Charles Lahy - Carlow	1788
Lahy, Thomas	Joey	510	416	332001	Thomas Lahy of Aughakilmore and Terence Joey of Aughakilmore (Publican). 10 Acres in Aughakilmore for 41 years yearly rent of £1 8s 31/2 d	1797 Full Trans
Lahy, John	Vaughan	496	84	318174	John Lahy of Carlow. Hercules Vaughan and Margaret Vaughan (Spinster) married John Lahee.	1795
Lahy, John		497	472	327140	Tallenture town, Carlow	
Lahy, Thomas		493	94	319919	14/7/1793 Rent Charges Made between Thomas Lahy and John Lahy of Aughakilmore Lower of one part and Patt Kilroy of Killeadreen of the other part – sum of £20 on day and timing shown until the sum of £80 16s 4d shall be fully paid off. The said Thomas & John Lahy tenants to be charged with non-payment charges if non-payment happens. Witnessed by Thomas McDowell of Kalenagh and John Kilroy of Killydrean.	1793
Leahy,	Collins	513	156	335765	John Leahy, Co Kerry.	1790

John						
Leahy, John		514	279	336394	Fowler and Ann Leahy of Cork	1798

1800-1809

From	To	Book No	Page No	Memorial No	Notes	
William Lahy	Strong	525	394	345139	Henry Strong of Tawlaught on behalf of his son Thomas Strong of the one part and William Lahy of Clonloaghan (Drumlumman) on behalf of his daughter Margaret Lahy of the other part. That [*James ?*] Strong did take to be his married wife the Pillaig Lahy & In consideration of marriage the said William Lahy did pay onto the said James Strong the sum of £100 as a marriage portion with his daughter Marg Lahy. Henry gives James half his lands in Tawlaught and the whole of the lands at his decease. If Margaret shall die without male or female issue in 6 years, then James Strong should return one half of the £100 to William Lahy. If Margaret shall die with no male heir & only female heirs then the sum of £100 should be paid to the heir or heirs of Tawlaught. If Margaret shall outlive James Strong then she shall be paid £10 yearly out of the lands of Tawlaught during her natural	1796

					life. Witnessed by Antony Kilroy of Killaduan & William Strong of Tawlaught & Henry Strong	
Richard Lahy	Maxwell	534	7	348967	Rick (Richard) Lahy of Aughakilmore (but now of Mount Nugent) and the late Henry Maxwell. £1465 lands (72 acres arable land and 5 acres bog) in Aughakilmore *Difficult to read*	1800
John Lahy	Lahee	555	200	370942	John Lahee of Carlow & mother and Sarah and Jane Lahee	1801
John Lahy	Rivers	553	539	370912	John Lahy of Tyloghny co Kilkenny & Michael Rivers of Carrick co Tipperary.	1803
Dorcas ? Lahy	Mancily	574	522	391569	Robert Stratford of Mancy Westmeath and Francis Lahy son and Dorcas Lahy widow of John Lahy of Williamstown and Ann Lahy Daughter of said John. (£250 Dowry) £30 to Ann Stratford. Witnessed by Robert Johnson and Patt Lahy.	1803
Henry Lahy	Gilroy	579	118	388775	Henry Lahy of Capragh and Anthony. Gilroy of Granard. Henry in consideration of £220 was lent and advanced a further sum of 5 shillings 14 Acres in Capragh for 500 years witnessed by Pat Brady and xxx Murphy and John O Reilly.	1805
Michael Lahy	Dyer	576	252	389173	Michael Lahy and Alia (Wife) and N. Walpole and Ann (Wife) both of New Birmingham Co Tipperary	1805
Richard Lahee		601	44	407716	Caddlestown, Kildare	1802
Charles Lahy		566	444	384399	Charles Lahy of Carlow	1796
Henry Lahy	Articles	577	524	390529	Henry Lahy of Capragh (Yeoman) and Jane Lahy of Aughakilmore in said County, Widow of the other part reciting articles entered into by the said	1805

					Henry and Jane Lahy bearing date 4th day of June last and consisting of several covenants and agreements....concerning town and lands of Upper Aughakilmore and Lower Aughakilmore....shall be lawful for said Jane and her children to enter into premises and use half part of the lands of Upper and Lower Aughakilmore and the rent and profits etc.. to which said Henry Lahy is entitled, should be subject to the payment of half such debts.... Contracted or created by the different persons of the name of Lahy (and Jane's children which when reach age of 21 will also be subject to this agreement).Witnessed by Andrew Bell Esq and Owen Keogh.	
Anne Lahy ?						
Michael Lahy & Wife		603	178	410694		
James Lahy						

1810-1812

From	To	Book No	Page No	Memorial No	Notes	
Patrick Lahy & wife		646	68	442053	Patrick Lahy and Wife (Jane) and Mary Cruise - Kildare	1812
John Lahy	Meighan	629	254	431938	Kilkenny	1810
Sarah Lahy	Carter	637	398	439239		
Francis Lahy	Strong	648	261	443664	Francis Lahy of Lavagh to James Strong of Tawlaught (*Difficult to read*)	1799

Lahee Sarah	Sikes	648	144	442349		
Lahee Charles	O Brien	650	582	447507		
Lahee John	Sikes	648	144	442349		
Lahee John	Williams	642	476	444990		

1813-1815

From	To	Book No	Page No	Memorial No	Notes	
William Lahy	Carvoll	659	301	456022	William Lahy of ofthinks in Co Kerry	
Michael Lahy	Hunt	659	338	456041	Michael Lahy of New Birmingham co Tipperary. Witnessed by Richard Lahy	
Clorwfe Lahy	Doyle	663	327	456198		
Francis Lahy & Wife	Gallaghahan	664	81	456417	Francis Lahy formerly of Lavagh and Rebecca Lahy his wife and John Galligan and Henry Burrows (Rebecca's brother ?). Witnessed by Henry McCabe, Arnold Lahy of Lavagh and Pat Brady.	1809
Francis & Wife –]Numbers wrong]	Bell	678	476	464617		

1816-1818

From	To	Book No	Page No	Memorial No	Notes	
Pat Lahiff	Hagan	699	536	479711	Pat Lahiff, Mill St, Limerick to Denis Hagan (Publican)	1814

Francis Lahy, Rebecca Burrows, Hannah	Marr	698	183	478911	Marriage Articles (Peter Brady & Hannagh Lahy) Peter Brady of Pullakell and John Brady of Pullakell Francis Lahy of Lavagh, Hannagh Lahy daughter of said Francis and Rebecca and Steward Mulligan of Corsmullo and Hugh Brady of Oldcastle Peter Brady gave land to Steward and Hugh, lands of Garnasallagh and Pullakeel. Francis and Rebecca together with their said daughter lands to Steward and Hugh Brady – lands of Lavagh (70 Acres) and lands leased by Col John Brady – 200 acres and lands of Killymullen and Corsumalla - £20 yearly paid to Hannagh for Life. Witnessed by Patrick McCabe of Lavagh	1814
Thomas Lahy	Fogarty	715	152	89087	Thomas Lahy of Thurle Co Tipperary	1811
Richard Lahee		725	369	95305	Richard Lahy of Naus – Kildare and John Lahee of Kilmonack, Kildare	

1819-1821						
From	**To**	**Book No**	**Page No**	**Memorial No**	**Notes**	
Francis Lahy, Rebecca Burrows, Jane Lahy	Articles	736	131	501666	Pat Mc Cabe and Francis Lahy of Lavagh –& Wife (Rebecca Burrows) and Jane Lahy 4th daughter of Francis and Rebecca, spinster of the 70 Acres £370. Jane Lahy mentioned	1819 (begun 1815)

					(daughter ?). Witnessed by Arnold Lahy of Knocknaheen Co Cavan	
Pat Sheehan	Jeremiah Lahy	745	201	507136	Pat Sheehan of Waterford, farmer and Jeremiah Lahy of Kilkenny, land in city of Waterford	1819
Patrick Lahy	John Lahy	761	316	516851	Marriage articles. Pat Lahy of Drumeeny and John Lahy (Son). Harriet Strong and William Strong of Killeshandra and James Strong of Tawlaught. £300 dowry to Pat Lahy and 10 shillings to James Strong and Land in Aughakilmore to John. Witnessed by Christopher Robinson and John Brady	1821 FULL TRAN

1822-1824

From	To	Book No	Page No	Memorial No	Notes	
Lahee, Sarah	Thornton	782	425	529560		
Lahee	Baker	783	197	529932		
Lahy, Mary		791	63	534598		

1825-1827

From	To	Book No	Page No	Memorial No	Notes	
Edmund Lahey	Kennedy	808	163	544898		
Timothy Lahey	Lahy	799	120	539453	Timothy Lahy – Kilkenny (1825) Craddockstown to John Lahy (Craddockstown)	
Lahey, Henry	***	811	587	547122		
Lahey, Edward		817	431	550556		

Lahey, James	**	811	387	547122		
Lahy, Mary, James	***	811	587	547122		
Lahy, John	***	821	349	552884		

1828

From	To	Book No	Page No	Memorial No	Notes	
John Lahy	Articles	833	293	560028	John Packenham Lahy and Anne Stafford, widow and executor of will of Robert Stafford. Marriage to be had between Anne Stafford and John Lahy. £800. The lands of cabrah (Caprah ?) in the county of Cavan. Yearly sum of £100. Witnessed by Patrick Lahy of Drumeeny (gentleman) and Michael Byrne of amesgrow, Westmeath.	1828
Cloff on	Walker	836	377	561912		

1828-32

From	To	Book No	Page No	Memorial No	Notes	
Lahie, Anne	McAllester	866	187	576687		
Lahie, Anne		885	64	586064		
Lahey, Michael	Dwyer	877	21	582021		
Lahiff, Thomas		878	393	582893		
Lahy, Thomas	Michen	884	223	585723		
Lahy, Thomas		890	461	588961		
Henry Lahy	William & George Lahy				Henry Lahy (Sen) of Capragh and William and George (a minor) his brother (sons). Henry owns 27	1831

					acres in Capragh. £240 to be paid to the sons. Witnessed by: Thomas Lahy of Aughakilmore, James Lahy of Tawlaught, Henry Lahy of Clonloaghan George Carmichael, Dublin Charles McCreedy of Dublin	

1833-1839

From	To	Book No	Page No	Memorial No		Notes
John Lahy	Webb	1	273	155	1835	
Susanna John George William Henry James Anne	Articles	10	155	155	1836	All of the 'Capragh' line. FULL TRAN

1840-1849

From	To	Book No	Page No	Memorial No	Notes	
Patrick Lahy	Landers (Pat)	23	286		Patrick & Richard Lahy from Tipperary - Ballydouough	

1850-59

From	To	Book No	Page No	Memorial No	Notes	
Moore	Patrick Lahy				Samuel Moore of the Rocks aged 30, William Pollock of Corstruce, Freeman Strong of Tawlaught, Patrick Lahy of Lislea. Obtained a judgement in her Majesty's court of common pleas for sum of £1000, £3, 2s 8d Pat Lahy in possession (Illegally ?) of the townlands of Aughaconny. And that £207 s14 3d still remains partly due to Samuel Moore as per agreement	22/3/1853
Moore	Patrick Lahy				Samuel Moore of the Rocks did on 22/3/1853 obtain a judgement against William Pollock of Costuce collector for Barony of Clonmahon, Freeman Strong of Tawlaught and Patrick Lahy of Lislea and in the course herein after mentioned for the sum of £1000 debt leases and £3 2s & 8d costs, £207 14s 3d still owing	1857
Lahy	Hamilton	33	210		William Lahy of Edrowora and John Hamilton of Aghacreevy. William owns land in Capragh containing the Police barracks.	6/8/1857

					William Lahy applied for loan of £147 10s Granted one accurity yearly rent charges of £15 to be paid out of the land and Police barracks and paid onto John Hamilton and his heirs *(Previous covenants mentioned)* Mathew Tully (Witness ?)	
Lahy	Heaney	11	227		Henry Heaney of Aughafad, William Lahy of Edermowin. Heany obtained a judgement in her Majesty's court of the Exchequer for sum of £39 17s, besides £37 14s 4d for costs. Respondent (Heaney) usual place of abode Aughorahadonna in county of Cavan. William is in Edermin. William owns land in Capragh. £27 1ss 10d to be secured by said judgement.	5/4/1859
Lahy	Mee				John Lahy of Aughakilmore . Henry his eldest son and Sophie Mee of Ennishmore, William Mee and Henry Mee son of William. John Gave 13 acres of Upper Aughakilmore to Henry & his heirs forever. Permits Henry to access dwelling and 10 acres of swill lands.	Jan 1857

					£45 Dowry paid by William Mee to Henry. Henry got all Upper Aughakilmore bounded by lands of Clonmahon and Tawlaught comprising about 13 acres and then in occupation of William Lahy. 5s paid will William Mee to Henry. £12 as yearly rent for said 13 acres. Witness Thomas Lahy of Lower Aughakilmore & Henry Mee of Drumeeny and George Mee.	
William Lahy					Mortgage Deed. William Lahy of Edermin, Frances Lahy (otherwise Kemp) wife of William& Patrick Donocho of Drummlumin. Sold Capragh (14 acres) for £120 12s. Witnesses, Patrick Leddy of Ardlang, Patrick Caffney of Cavan	14/3/1857
Lahey	Tallow	40		298	John Tallow of 49 Fleet St Dublin & William Lahey of Edermin Amount recovered is £120 16s 2d and £7 4s 11d costs. William owns lands in Capragh and sum of £28 1s 1d still remains partly due.	Dec 1859

1850-1859						
From	To	Book No	Page No	Memorial No	Notes	
Leahy	O Reilly	12		10	6/12/1848 Patrick Leahy of Derrin and	1851

					Jane O Reilly of Lislin (Widow) & Thomas Leahy of Drumeeny and John Brady of Lavagh.	FULL TRAN
Wood	Leahy	29		92	31/8/1855 Margaret Wood of Clonloaghan (Widow), Robert Wood her son of Clonloaghan of 2nd part, Thomas Leahy of Drumeeny and Sarah Leahy spinster his daughter & Thomas Carty Goff of Oldcastle & Rev Mathew Webb of Omard. Marriage between Robert Wood and Sarah Leahy. Farm of Margaret & Robert Wood to be held by Thomas Cart Goff & Mathew Webb as trustees. Lower Aughakilmore – 15 Acres, 3 Roods & 31 Perches to hold for 100 years. Margaret Wood to get £16 yearly pension from said lands. If Sarah survives Robert she gets £12 per year. Witnessed by Patrick Leahy & John Brady.	1855
Leahy	Close	16		7	Patrick Leahy of Great Brunswick Street Dublin Vs Close George Close of Upper Kevin St on 26/11/1846 did obtain a judgement in her Majesty's Court of the Queens Bench against Patrick Leahy of Great Brunswick Street for the sum of £305 1s 11d. Patrick known to be in possession of property at 12	1855

					Great Brunswick Street [detailed measurements] £150 from said judgment remains outstanding. Witness Thomas Byron attorney 59 Upper Mount Street	
Rotheram	Leahy	19		165	2/6/1858 Marriage Settlement Between Thomas Rotheram of Tiermore, Meath and Elizabeth Jane Leahy of Crover and Edward Rotheram of Crossdrum, Meath Esq Junior and James Leahy Esq surgeon in the Royal Navy. Edward is the father to Thomas Rotheram and owns lands in Martinstown, Westmeath. Lands left to him by his father's will dated 1813 and upon marrying to Elizabeth, charges to be made on said lands of Martinstown of £200 a year for Elizabeth Leahy, in lieu of dowry in case she should survive him. Witnessed by James Leahy, junior, Samuel Gerrard of Lower Ormond Quay Dublin, solicitor and Charles Malone of Upper Rutland Street Dublin.	1858
Henry Lahy	William Lahy	39		289	Henry Lahy senior of Capragh & William Lahy for himself and also in trust for George Lahy his brother – a minor – both lawful sons of said Henry Lahy of Capragh. Henry owns 27 acres in Capragh to sons in consideration of £240 paid	1859

					by William and George. Witnessed by Thomas Lahy of Aughakilmore, James Strong of Tawlaught & Henry Lahy of Clonloaghan & George Carmichael of Lower Dominic Street Dublin & Charles McCready of Richmond (clerk to Carmichael)	
William Lahy	Donadio	14		55	30/4/1859 - William Lahy of Edmon	1859

1860-1870

From	To	Book No	Page No	Memorial No	Notes	
Leahy	Goff	18		281	15/5/1862 Between Thomas Leahy of Drumeeny, Cavan and Maria Goff of Oldcastle, Meath, widow and Richard O'Neill of Oldcastle (auctioneer) Thomas Lahy bought from Richard O Neill (at the request of Maria Goff) for £400 the plot of ground in the town of Oldcastle formerly in the possession of Robert Wilson and lately in the possession of Thomas Goff demised by a certain judge of demise 1/10/1843. Annuity rent charge of £15 payable to Maria Goff for life. Witnessed by John C Goff of Moate, Meath and John	1862

					Thomas of Westmoreland Street, Dublin.	
Lahy	Sheridan	16		271	Lucinda Lahy and James Sheridan Marriage Articles – father = Patrick Lahy of Mountdutton. Patrick Lahy of Aughakilmore and Eleanor his wife and Richard Marsh and wife Catherine Marsh (otherwise Lahy). John Brady of Lavagh and Thomas Lahy of Drumeeny. Rev John Sheridan owns 60 acres in Ballina and Patrick Lahy owned 1/3 part of the lands of Aghaconny. £200 to be paid by James Sheridan to Patrick. John Sheridan gave ½ his lands in Ballina and ½ the bog in Lavagh. Aghaconny lands – Patrick permits James Sheridan to lift the rents from Aghaconny leases of less than 31 years during his natural life. If Lucinda survives James she receives £20. Witnesses Daniel Sheridan, Thomas Sheridan.	1865
Mary Lahy	Christopher Radcliff	14		73	Mary Leahy, of 22 Richmond street to marry Christopher Radcliffe of Malahide. Mary got £60 / year from Will of James McFadden formerly of	1866

					Stephens Green – payable from the lands in Sligo and Cavan: Cavan Lands: Leam(Clonmahon) Drumhannagh, Drumsillagh, Drumcalpin, Stroone, Upper & Lower Loagtree	
Rotheram to Leahy		11		226	12/4/1866 Between John Adolphus Leahy of Williamstown Westmeath and Elizabeth Jane Rotheram of 28 Holles Street Dublin, widow, James Wilton Leahy of Melville Hospital, Chatham, England, surgeon of the Royal Navy of 3rd Part. Reciting earlier deed 2/6/1858 between Thomas Rotheram (deceased) and Elizabeth Jane Rotheram (otherwise Leahy) and Edward Rotheram and said James Wilton Leahy. Receives all lands of Martinstown in the barony of Delvin in the county of Westmeath. Elizabeth to get £200 per year rent, charged from said lands – to go to James Wilton Leahy if she dies. Witnessed William Parsons & John Taylor of No 7 Dawson Street (solicitor).	1866
John Adolphus Leahy	Sidney	29		239	13/10/1866 Between John Adolphus Leahy of 28 Holles Street Dublin and James Waller Sidney of 6 Russel Place	1866

					Dublin Reference Lease 29/4/1865, James Waller Sidney set unto Elizabeth Jane Rotheram of Novara, Bray in the county of Wicklow, widow all that message or tenement known as No 28 Holles Street together with the coach house and stable and garden on east side of the street in manor of Baggot street parish of Saint Peter and county of Dublin to hold to the said Elizabeth Jane Rotheram for 10 years from June 1st at yearly rent of £50 and further reciting that a marriage was duly had and solemnised between the said John Adolphus Leahy and Elizabeth Jane Rotheram on 13/4/1866. John Adolphus surrendered up onto James Waller Sidney No 28 Holles Street.	

1870-1879

From	To	Book No	Page No	Memorial No	Notes	
William Lahy	McGivney	11		14	29/3/1870 Between John Lahy of Aughakilmore and William son of said John Lahy and Henry and Thomas Lahy – sons of said John – all of Aughakilmore and Philip	1870

					McGivney of Kilnaleck (merchant). £539 12s 8d owing to said Philip by the said William Lahy and a further sum of £40 7s 4d, the balance of a sum of £280 the purchase money so agreed of said lands aforesaid to the said William Lahy this day paid by the said Philip McGivney. The Lahys gave part of Aughakilmore now in possession of James Galligan and Richard Fitzsimmons (as tenants to said William Lahy). John and William did grant unto Philip McGivney Henry and Thomas land containing 8 acres and 37 perches. Witnessed by John Sheridan of Kilnaleck, shopkeeper, John Fanelly of Kilnaleck – law clerk and Anne Lahy otherwise Stephens, wife of said William Lahy.	
Henry Lahy	McGivney	11		15	29/3/1870 Between John Lahy of Aughakilmore and William son of said John Lahy and Henry and Thomas Lahy – sons of said John – all of Aughakilmore and Philip McGivney of Kilnaleck (merchant). £59 owing to Philip McGivney and further sum of £141 agreed upon to be advanced by the said Philip McGivney – thus £200 in total paid by the said Philip McGivney to the said Henry Lahy.	1870

					With interest of £6 per gent per annum. Doth grant unto Philip McGivney all those lands in Upper and Lower Aughakilmore in the possession tenancy or occupation of said John, Henry, William and Thomas or their under tenants.	
		11		16	29/3/1870 Between John Lahy of Aughakilmore and William son of said John Lahy and Henry. Thomas Lahy – sons of said John – all of Aughakilmore and Philip McGivney of Kilnaleck (merchant). £95 Owing and a further £160 owing on advance to Philip McGivney. Total = £225	1870
Leahy	Donohoe	12		25	10/4/1867. Patrick Leahy of Aughakilmore, shopkeeper and farmer and Patrick Donahoe of Druminiskilin in county of Cavan. £250 owed to Pat Donahoe by Pat Leahy released rent charges of £30 for the term of 12 years from Nov 1st 1866 until said sum of £250 was paid off. Patrick Leahy (since deceased) is witnessed by John Leddy of Ardleny and Thomas Keogh of Gortnaleck (Leitrim) and Ellen Donohoe otherwise McBreen the widow of said Patrick Donohoe, since deceased. Witnessed by John Leddy and Edmund Kelly of Cavan, law clerk.	1873
Lahey	Gilchrist	51		20	Affidavit to register judgement as a mortgage,	1874

					court of the Queens bench. John Gilchrist of Finea shopkeeper aged 30+ for the sum of £27 12s 10d besides the sum of £7 4s 11d thus a total of £34 17s 9d. Former case. Thomas Gilchrist (deceased) and Robert Thomas Leahy, trade = Esquire. Part of the lands of Moydristan otherwise Moate containing 92 acres, 9 perches and other lands in Moydristan containing 69 acres 1 rood and 5 perches. Signed at Castlepollard.	
Leahy	Phair	26		288	22/6/1874. John Phair of Main Street, Killeshandra paid £93 to Margaret Leahy of Coragh Glebe in Cavan, widow for all lands of Coragh Glebe in the barony of Tullyhunco, containing 5 acres 2 roods and 13 perches.	1874
Lahy	Wood	14		122	14/3/1876.Robert Wood and Sarah Wood otherwise Leahy of Aughakilmore. Sarah relinquishes her £12 a year pension from deed dated 31/8/1855. Witnessed by Edward McGauran, solicitor and Terence Caldwell.	1876
Lahy	Sheridan	32		187	19/7/1877. Mortgage between John Leahy of Aughakilmore, Gentleman and James Sheridan of Ballina Esq. John did grant onto James all the lands of Aughakilmore now in possession of John and his under tenants. Witnessed by Hugh P Kennedy of Cavan, Solicitor and William Cassidy of Cavan (clerk)	1877

1880-1889

From	To	Book No	Page No	Memorial No	Notes	
Leahy	Sheridan	1880			28/2/1880. John Leahy of Aughakilmore, Esquire and James Sheridan of Ballina. In consideration of £300, $175 and £75 was already due and owing by the said John Leahy to the said James Sheridan and the residue thereof namely £175 at the date of execution of the said deed paid to the said John Leahy by the said James Sheridan – the receipt of which is acknowledged. The said John Leahy has entered into a covenant that he (John) would pay James Sheridan the sum of £300 with interest at the rate of £5 10s percent per annum on 1st November next without any deduction and then John did grant onto James Sheridan all his lands in Aghakilmore. Witnessed Daniel Sheridan of Ballina and Michael Cassidy of Aughafad (Farmer).	1880
Thomas Lahy	Philip McGivney	1881		237	5/8/1881 – Thomas Lahy 1st Part, William and Henry Lahy of 2nd Part, All of Aughakilmore, and Philip McGivney of 3rd part. Sold McGivney two plots of land, 1. 5 Acres and 3 roods currently in possession of John Masterson	1881

					2. 4 acres 1 rood. Witnessed by William Cassidy and Michael Reilly.	
Henry Lahy	Philip McGivney	1881		238	9/8/1881.Henry, William and Thomas Lahy of Aughakilmore – sold land in Lower Aughakilmore: Two plots: 1. 5 acres, 3 roods and 34 perches as now in possession of Hugh Coyle and 2. 3 Acres 2 roods and 14 perches in possession of Henry Lahy. Witnessed by William Cassidy of Cavan (law clerk) and Michael Reilly of Kilnaleck (shop assistant)	1881
Ernest Garibaldi Leahy	John Adolphus Leahy	1882		55	25/1/1882. Ernest in possession of lands worth £80 – Sold Williamstown (70 acres) to John Adolphus Leahy. Witnessed by Samuel Mooney % William Lawlor of 37 Westmoreland St, Dublin.	1882
Land judges	McLoughlin & Leahy		34	74	8/8/1883.John Gordon Leahy – a minor – in consideration of £1000 ascertained by the court in respect of the surplus after payment of rembrances affecting the estate of Robert J Leahy owner as part, Michael J Barter and other parishioners authorized to be retained by Ellen McLaughlin of Abbeyleix in Queens county, widow – the guardian of the person and	1883

					fortune of the said John Gordon Leahy a minor in charge of the purchase money of £1000. Part of the lands of Moydristan containing 69 acres 1 rood and 5 perches as described in witnessed map together with a right of way for said Ellen McLaughlin which passes that other part of the lands of Moydristan otherwise Moate purchased in said manner by George Porter of Oldcastle (Merchant). Made between George Porter 1st part, Bridget Smith and others the 2nd Part and Ellen McLaughlin and said John Gordon Lahey of the 3rd part and Pshing Clarke and other of the 4th part – and list of tenants – Judge Henry Ormby.	
Lahy	Lahy	31		167	31/7/1883. George Lahy of Capragh – 1st part, Mary Anne Lahy wife of said George 2nd part and John William Lahy farmer and his wife Harriet – both of Capragh. In consideration of £50 to George from John William, George did grant onto the said Mary Anne Lahy 15 acres of Capragh for the term of her natural life – then onto John William and Harriet. Witnessed Richard Allen of Cavan and Witnessed Henry Clarke, clerk to Richard Allen Solicitor. – By signing his name as	1883

					George 'Leahy' which is meant for and is one and the same as 'George Lahy' and John William and Harriet Lahy, otherwise Lahey.	
Leahy	Sheridan	26		54	16/5/1884. John Leahy of 1st part, Elinor Leahy of 2nd part and James Sheridan of Ballina of 3rd part. John did grant onto James lands in Aughakilmore now in possession of Con. Sheridan and William Leahy (under tenants) and Elinor releases all claims in other deeds entitling her to £17 per year. Witness Peter Lawlor of Cavan, Solicitor and Owen Caldwell law Clerk.	1884
Lahy	Land Commission	12		119	27/2/1885. John Leahy of 1st part – The 'tenant'. Commissioners of Public works incorporated by the statute 10 & 11 Victoria Cap 32 and acting in execution of the land law (Ireland) act 1881 and of the landed property improvement (Ireland) acts as defined by the said land law act (Ireland) 1881…. The said tenant in pursuance of the agreement therein mentioned and in consideration of £150 to be lent as therein mentioned did the rely charge that part of the lands of Williamstown and Cornacreevy in his occupation situate in the barony of Fore in the	1885

					county of Westmeath and all his tenancy estate and interest therein with the payment to the said commissioners or their assigns for all advances from time to time made to him by the said commissioners with interest on said advances at the rate therein mentioned and he did thereby covenant therein which said Indenture as to the execution thereof by the said tenant is witnessed by the Rev. R. Archdall Byrn of Drumcree in the county of Westmeath, Clerk, Minor Robinson of Robinstown in the county of Westmeath aforesaid Gentleman and Frederick Leahy of 30 Upper Georges Street, Kingstown in the county of Dublin and Gentleman John Leahy [seal]. At Granard in the county of Longford on Justice of the peace for Co Longford R. Stafford Tuite.	
Lahy	Hamilton	15		134	6/4/1886. William Lahy of Mullaghboy (farmer) and Margaret Lahy his wife and Henry Lahy of Clonloaghan (farmer). Reciting Mortgage dated 6/8/1857 between William Lahy since deceased of the one part and John Hamilton since deceased of the second part to secure the payment of £127 10s as therin charged	1886

					on the premises and that the estate of the said William Lahy deceased is now vested in the said Henry Lahy and all the estate of said John Hamilton deceased is now vested in said William Lahy and Margaret Lahy said indenture of which this is a memorial witnessed for the considerations therein the said William and Margaret Lahy his wife as Mortgagees did grant and convey onto the said Henry Lahy his heirs and assigns all that and premises at present occupied as a police barracks situate in the lands of Capragh together with a yearly rent of £15. Witnessed Richard Allen, Solicitor and William Henry Clarke (clerk).	
Lahy	Simons	38		20	Mortgage. Henry Lahy of Cavan and James Simons of Cavan (Auctioneer). Henry Lahy in Fee and some other good after sufficient estate of inheritance. James Simons has advanced at different times sums amounting to £230. Henry signs over to James Simons all lands of Capragh in possession of Henry and his under tenant Michael Donohoe containing 14 acres and the house at present occupied as a police barracks together with a yearly rent of £15.	1886

					Witnessed by William Henry Healpin of 24 dame St Dublin – aged 21 and Richard Allen of Cavan, Solicitor.	
Lahy	Beattie	43		65	Judgement Mortgage, 1st October 1886. Judgement Mortgage Act 139 14 Vic c. 29 1886 M230 is In the high court of Justice, Ireland, Exchequer Dublin. Between William Beattie plaintiff and Henry Lahy defendant. William Beattie of 13 Main St Cavan (shopkeeper) for the sum of £46 9s 2d besides the sum of £12 1s 3d for cash making together £58 10s 5d. Henry of Cavan in County Cavan profession 'Gentleman'. Henry in possession of lands in Capragh containing 14 acres and house presently occupied as police barracks. The sun of £58 10s 5d still remains due besides interest at the rate of £4 percent per annum.	1886
Lahy	RIC	10		143	3/3/1887. Henry Lahy of Cavan in the county of Cavan, Gentleman and Andrew Keed Esq of Dublin Castle receiver for the Constabulary Force of Ireland. The house together with the right of way over the avenue leading from the said house and premises to the public road situate on the East side of said premises and leading from Kilcogy to Kilnaleck, for term of	1887

					21 years from 31/12/1886 at yearly rent of £18. Witnessed by Richard Allen of Cavan, Solicitor and William henry Clarke – solicitors clerk.	
Leahy	Kelly	53		109	10/12/1886. David Leahy, William Kelly & Jeremiah Leahy all of Belfast – Tobacco & Snuff Dealers. Mortgages, James McAuley publican of 2nd part and Nicolas Hughes of Coleraine grocer and wine merchant. Dwelling house yard and premises on west side of Nelson St, No 114, Belfast	1886
Simons	Vance	12		154	7/3/1887. Simons and Vance and William Vance of Earlsvale (auctioneer) grants onto William Vance all lands in Capragh now in the possession of Michael Donoghue (tenant) for a judicial term and yearly rent of £10 10s. Witnessed by Samuel Jones, Solicitor and William Henry Clarke.	1887
Lahy	Simons & Beattie	12		142	James Simons (of the 1st part) of Cavan (auctioneer) and Saddler, Henry Lahy of Cavan (2nd part) (Gentleman) and William Beattie (of 3rd part) (shopkeeper). £230 paid by James Simons to Henry and Henry did grant deeds to him – Mortgage 11 Sept 1886. have been paid. £185 paid to Henry Lahy by William Beattie. All lands in possession of RIC and the barracks. Witnessed by Richard	1887

| | | | | | Allen solicitor and Samuel Jones of Cavan, solicitor. | |

1890-99

From	To	Book No	Page No	Memorial No	Notes	
Leahy	McVeigh	82		20	5/11/1898. Emily McVeigh (Wife of Hugh McVeigh) of Ballynahinch [publican] and Robert John Leahy of Ballynahinch. In previous deed (1887) William Leahy conveyed all this estate and interest in the tenements and premises therein.	1898
Leahy	Building Society	63		39	Frederick Leahy of 27 Ballybough road, Dublin and Hannah Mary Leahy, his wife. Mortgage of £400 to Building Society.	1899

1900-1910

From	To	Book No	Page No	Memorial No	Notes	
Lahy	Knox	5		200	30/12/1899. An indenture of marriage settlement between William Lahey of Killyfassey, Cavan, farmer and Robert Knox of Killyfassey, Methodist minister of 2nd part and Eva Lahey of Killyfassey of 3rd part (spinster) and William Strong of Turin House of the 4th part. William signs over his farm in Killyfassey containing 47 acres. To William strong executor to hold for his natural life and then to Robert Knox. If Eva dies without issue then Robert Knox must give up the farm and receive £200. Witnessed by Mary Anne Strong	1900

					(married woman) and Frances J. Strong (spinster) both of Fortview, Ballyjamesduff.	
Leahy	Foster	56		80	Joseph Foster of Kilmainham (farmer), Jane Lahey of Aughakilmore (spinster) and Bernard Brady of Kilcogy. Sum of £330 paid by Bernard Brady to the said Jane Leahy, he the said Joseph Foster as personal representative of William Wesley and the said Jane Leahey as beneficial did sign onto Bernard Brady the town and lands of Clonloaghan, containing 50 acres, 1 rood and 38 perches. Witnessed by William John Fegan, solicitor and Joe Fegan, Solicitors.	1900
Leahy		57		73	John Leahy of Castle Street, Dalkey, Dublin, Merchant and Thomas Kelly of Colmore Road, Dalkey	1900
Leahy		41		182	William Leahy of Ardakipmore Dunnahure, Leitrim (16 acres, 2 Roods, 26 Perches)	1902
Leahy		80		43	18 acres, 0 Roods, 30 perches – lands of Ardakipmore, barony of Drumahore, Leitrim. Frank Lahy of Arkakipmore.	1902
Leahy		45		119	Armagh. William Flanagan and William Leahy (painter) and Elizabeth Jane Leahy, his wife, both of Edenaveys, Co Armagh £170 Mortgage for 18 acres in Drungreagh.	1903
Leahy	Leahy	5		79	John Henry Leahy of Brookfield in the colony of Queensland, Australia of the one part and Harriett Leahy, wife of John William Leahy of Capragh. In consideration of the sum of £100 paid by the said Harriett Leahy to the said John Henry Leahy (receipt acknowledged). All that part of the lands of Capragh containing 22 acres 1 rood and 4	1903

					perches, formerly in the possession of Henry Lahy to which George became entitled as tenant intestate under the provisions of an indenture dated 26/1/1831. Also subject to a charge of £60 payable to Elizabeth Cassidy to hold some units and to the use of said Harriet Cassidy her heirs etc.. Witnessed by William Lawlor, Brisbane Solicitor.	
Leahy	Leahy	5		80	Between Harriet Leahy of Capragh, wife of John William Leahy – the Mortgagees and Julia Leahy of Aughakilmore, wife of John Leahy (of same place). Agreed to lend the sum of £100 for the purchase of Capragh, - 22 acres, 1 rood and 4 perches.	1903
Lahey	Council	32		250	William Strong of Turin house, William Lahey of Killyfassey and the Cavan rural district council. William Lahey granted lands in Killyfassey containing 2 roods and 10 perches. Witnessed by Robert Crove, solicitors clerk and Joseph Fegan, Solicitor of Cavan	1905
Leahy	Metcalfe	29		76	16/3/1906. Francis Metcalf of Metcalf Park, Enfield Co Kildare and John white Leahy of Laieth, Killarney in Co of Kildare, Esquire. Mortgages give to John Mac Guillycuddy, mansion house and offices of Juilcagh and demesne, 61 acres, 15 perches being in the barony of Castlerahen, county Cavan – parish of Mullagh.	1906
		27		133	6/4/1907. Harriett Leahy of Capragh, wife of John William Leahy, John William of Capragh and Elizabeth Cassidy of Dungimmin, married woman of 3rd part, Elizabeth Cassidy junior of Capragh, spinster of 4th part,	1907

					Henry Heaney of Aghdooney 5th part and John Heaney of Aghadooney, farmer (the trustee). Intended marriage. She the said Harriett Leahy as beneficial owner did grant and convey onto the said John Heaney all the lands of Capragh containing 22 acres 1 rood and 4 perches. For use by Harriett during her natural life and then for the use of John William and then to Henry Heaney and Elizabeth Cassidy junior (his intended wife). £60 created in favour of said Elizabeth Cassidy. Witnessed Joe Fegan, solicitor and James Farrel, Clerk of Cavan. Witnessed by James Donohue of Garrison, farmer and Michael Donohue of Capragh.	
Lahey		20		183	16/2/1909. James Lahey (farmer) of Lavagh, Anne Walker of Kilnahard (spinster) and Joseph Walker of Kilnahard. Marriage to be had between James and Anne. 15 Acres in Lavagh from Joseph Walker (as dowry). Witness. John Fegan, Solicitor and James Farrell (clerk) of Cavan.	1909
Leahy	Leahy	29		249	2/3/1909. John Leahy of Williamstown and Stanley Leahy of Williamstown (son of said John). Stanley paid £600 to John for Williamstown farm of 160 acres & the young pony and trap and harness and 3 young calves and the furniture in the parlour, all our glass china, silver and electro plated articles in said parlour and also the piano in said dwelling house. Witnessed Henry N. Wacker of Cornacreevy, Finea and George Whyte of Kilgolagh,, Granard.	1909

1910-1920

From	To	Book No	Page No	Memorial No	Notes	
Leahy	Leahy	21		240	6/3/1914. Richard Leahy of Aughakilmore and Harriett Thompson of Dundalk, wife of Frederick Thompson of same place and sister of Richard Leahy.*[4 Acres of land and dwelling house given by Richard to his sister Harriet]* . Witnessed by Joseph Fagan Solicitor – Cavan.	1914
Leahy	Leahy	42		75	12/4/1915. Harriet Thompson, Frederick Thompson and Julia Leahy (wife of John). £66 14s 10d due by Harriet Thompson and Richard Leahy for goods sold and delivered and cash lent and a further sum of £83 5s 2d of advances giving a total of £150. Gave 4 acres of land [*the Cross ?*] to Julia. Witnessed by John Fegan, Solicitor.	1915
Leahy	Leahy	30		86	Harriett Thompson of Dundalk and Richard Leahy of Dundalk and Julia of Aughakilmore (wife of John). £100 paid by Julia together with a sum of £150, giving a total of £250. Richard Leahy and Hugh Weir subscribed as witness to said deed, containing 4 acres.	1916

1919-1930

From	To	Book No	Page No	Memorial No	Notes	
Robert Leahy	George William Leahy	8		134	23/12/1919. Robert Leahy of Mullaghboy, Harriet (wife) of said Robert and George William Leahy of Mullaghboy - son of said	1919

					Robert Leahy and Harriet. In consideration of an intended Marriage and sum of £300 paid by the said George William to the said Robert Leahy as beneficial owner doth hereby assign unto the said George William Leahy lands in Mullaghboy containing 29 acres and 21 Perches and buildings etc. Witnessed by Joseph Fegan, Solicitor, Cavan and Darry Vance (typist). Witnessed 24/1/1920.	
George William Leahy	Robert Leahy	33		284	8/4/1920. George William Leahy of Mullaghboy and Robert Leahy of Mullaghboy. George gives Robert 29 acres, 21 Perches together with dwellings, stock, chantells, furniture and tenants rights by virtue of an indenture assignment 23/12/1919. Witnessed James Mulseed (Solicitor) apprentice & Hugh McGovern (Solicitors clerk)	1920
Stanley Leahy	Land Commission	56		267	Schedule of Deeds Titles - 7433 Williamstown (A110, R0, P21) Cornacreevy (A41, R0, P37) Moneybeg (A4,R0, P9) Clareisland / Derrymuclgan (A1, R2, P20)	
John Leahy	Charles McClean	38		2	A memorial of an indenture of Marriage Settlement bearing the date the 22nd day of August nine hundred and twenty three and made between John Leahy senior of Aughakilmore in the county of Cavan farmer of the first part Julia Leahy of same place wife of the said John Leahy senior of the second part, John Leahy junior of the same place farmer of the third part and Charles McClean. - John and Anna May - Marriage Articles	1923 FULL TRAN
Robert Leahy	Pat Gafney	62		225	Robert Leahy of Mullaghboy and Pat Gafney of Lavagh. Sum of £1050 paid by Pat Gafney to said Robert Leahy. Robert sold farm of	1922

					32 acres. Rent from Captain Maxwell tenancy rate of £18. Witness Joe Fegan Solicitor	
John Leahy	George William Leahy	39		204	Between John Leahy (senior) Aughakilmore of 1st part, George William Leahy of the same place (farmer) of 2nd part and Stanley Leahy of Williamstown of 3rd Part. John gave unto Stanley land in Aghacreevy containing 36 acres & 39 Peches and houses & buildings etc.. to be held in trust for said George William Leahy in the event of George William becoming bankrupt then John and Julia hold the land in trust for claimant. Witnessed R. Haplin solicitor and Thomas Brady, Auctioneer.	1923
James Strong	Francis Leahy	24		277	1/6/1927. Between James Strong of Tawlaught and Francis Leahy of Drumeeny. £400 paid by Francis to James Strong and a further £100 for lands in Tawlaught containing 32 acres, 1 rood and 20 perches. Witnessed Joe Fegan, Solicitor Cavan and William Reid, Solicitor.	1927
George Small	Robert George Leahy	35		53	Robert George Leahy of Mullaghboy paid £550 and a further sum of £25 for a farm of 36 acres 3 roods owned by George Small of Mullaghboy. Witnessed	1927
George Leahy	Church	46		207	5/11/1929. George Leahy of Ballyheelan, Frederick Leahy of Drumeeny etc.. [list of other] 2 roods & 30 Perches of Land in Lavagh to the Church R.C.B. for land for a school.	1929
John Leahy	Thomas Cruise	17		64	John Leahy of Aughakilmore and Thomas Cruise of Clonoose. Tom Cruise paid £550 for land in Clonoose containing 43 acres 2 roods 11 perches. Witnessed Joe Fegan, Solicitor. Cavan	1929

1930-1940						
From	To	Book No	Page No	Memorial No	Notes	
Alexander and James Leahy	Young Leahy	14		30	Alexander Leahy of Ashley Cottage, Newcastle Co Down, Gardner and Edward Brady of Lavagh (Farmer) and James Leahy of Kilvaoe Lodge, Templagne in county of Dublin, Young Leahy of Ashfield, Cavan, Gardner. Young Leahy paid £70 to Alexander Leahy and Edwards Brady and further sum of £5 to said James Leahy. They (James Leahy and Alexander Brady) as seasonal representatives of the said William Leahy. Land containing 2 acres, 3 roods in Lavagh to Young Leahy. Witnessed by Robert Hanna of Castlewellanand Thomas John Hanna of Newcastle, George Grover (farmer) and Daisy Frazer (married woman) both of Crover, Mount Nugent and William McCullagh, Solicitor.	1931
John Leahy	Peter Pryor	32		124	30/6/1932. John Leahy of Aughakilmore, Executor of the will of Charles McClean late of Duffcastle and Alice	1932

					Marion Leahy, wife of the said William Leahy of Aghacreevy, Ballynarry and Peter Pryor of Duffcastle and Daphine, his wife. Peter and Daphine Pryor paid £490 to John Leahy at the request and direction of Alice Marion Leahy. John by direction from Alice Marion gave over to Peter Pryor from Duffcastle 27 Acres, 2 Roods, 10 Perches.	
John Leahy	Lucy McManus	35		111	31/10/1932. John Leahy of Aughakilmore (executor of Will of Charles McClean) and Anny May Leahy wife of said John & Lucy McManus of Mullaghboy Mount Nugent (married woman). Lucy McManus paid £130 to John Leahy as personal representative of Charles McClean did grant and convey onto the said Anna May Leahy did convey and confirm onto the said Lucy McManus all those premises granted in an Indenture of 30/12/1920. Land under occupation of Walter Smyth and representatives of William McKenna as sub-tenants of Charles McClean - lands	1932

From	To	Book No	Page No	Memorial No	Notes	
					situated in the town of Kilnaleck and right of way presently in occupation of James Gafney. Weekly Rents 5 shillings and 4 shillings.	
John Leahy	Hugh Coyle	28		157	John Leahy of Aughakilmore, Ballynarry (Farmer) and Hugh Coyle, Clonloaghan, Kilgogh. £262 10s for 4 acres Irish measure for land in Upper Aughakilmore. Witnessed. Joe Fegan.	1933
Robert George Leahy	Irish Land Commission	30		137	Collection No 143/2861 Reg No 83. Robert George Leahy, Mullaghboy. 36 Acres, 3 Roods, 0 Perches. Ref No 1 on Map. Judicial Agreement dated 28/2/1889. Standard Price £260	1939
Young Leahy	Irish Land Commission	30		137	Collection No 143/2884. Young Leahy, The Gardens, Ashfield Lodge, Cootehill, Cavan. Ref No 12 on Map - 3 (Lavagh) Acres, Price £20 10s, 6d. Ref No 13 on Map (Lavagh) 2 Acres, 3 Roods, 0 Perches. £34, 4s, 3d.	

1940-1960

From	To	Book No	Page No	Memorial No	Notes	
John Leahy	Ulster Bank	32		217	24/9/1940	1940

					John Leahy of Aughakilmore, Ballynarry, Kilnaleck, Publican and farmer & Ulster Bank Ltd, Waring Street, Belfast. Collateral security for full payment of money therein: Pottleboy (91 acres, 3 roods, 37 Perches) Garrison (82 acres, 3 roods, 18 perches) Old Garrison (26 acres, 28 perches) - formerly in the possession of James Charles Donohoe	
James Leahy	Land Commission	16		56	James Leahy of Aughakilmore . Collection 7/4. No on Map 5,7. Aughakilmore Lower farm (16 Acres, 1 rood, 39 perches). 27/7/1904. Price Purchase £104, 0s, 8d.	1946
John Leahy	Ulster Bank, Crover Farms	38		249	John Leahy of Aughakilmore 1st part, Ulster Bank of 2nd part and Crover Farms Ltd of 3rd part. £2000 for: Pottleboy (91 acres, 3 roods, 27 Perches). Garrison (56 acres, 2 roods, 30 perches) & Annuity of £26, 19s 10d payable to the Irish Land Commission. Witnessed by John C. Leahy of Aughakilmore and Louis Roche (Solicitors assistant).	1948
John Leahy	Thomas	61		205	John Leahy to Thomas	1950

	McEnroe				McEnroe (of Aughakilmore). Lower Aughakilmore 27 acres with licenced premises shop house and all buildings. Subject to yearly tithe rent charge of 7s 3d payable to the Irish Land Commission. 7 Day Licence attached. Witnessed Patrick Cusack, Ballyjamesduff, Solicitor and May Young, Typist.	

3 Lessee / Buyer

(Not listed in Names index above)

1708-1738

From	To	Book No	Page No	Memorial No	Notes	
Hampson	Smith	14	279	5078		
Hampson	Shapely					
Pollard						
Hampson	Wood	47	2	2987		
Pollard Hampson	Dowly					
Fitzpatrick	Lahy	82	280	57849	Rick Fitzpatrick of Derrin and Henry Lahy of Upper Aghakilmore, George Fitzpatrick and Ann (his wife). £ 120 10s for 25 acres in the lands of middle Aghakilmore formerly in the possession of George Fitzpatrick lands of the late John Fitzpatrick (deceased). Hocles Gardens Orchards, Cottages. In the presence of William Lahy, Oliver Cheevers, John Lahy and Thomas Lahy.	1735
Lahy	Lahy	82	458	58573	1719. John Lahy to William Lahy (Will & Dowry?) and Also To Mary Lahy (Daughter) and son in law William Heny of Tinway.	
Whiteetux	Sheridan	459				

1739-1810

From	To	Book No	Page No	Memorial No	Notes	
Heany	Lahy	96	50	66349	1738. John Lahy	
Lahy	Cheevers	201	???	192706		
Lahy	Lahy	338	271	227527	20/7/1764. Joseph Lahy Aughakilmore & Henry Lahy 2nd	1764

Lahy	Lahy	273	349	177861	son and heir. Debt 1773. £120	
Lahy	Lahy	273	349	177861	William Lahy of Lavagh. £240 Paid by James Lahy of Aghakilmore, lands in Lavagh and Aghacreevy in possession of Brian Coyle (undertennant) to Thomas Cheevers – 16 Acres. Witnessed by Thomas Lahy of Aghakilmore Lower and Rob Achessob of Dublin.	1769
Lahy	Cheevers	201	???	187074		

4   Full Transcriptions

Memorial No	From	To	Date
58573	John Lahy	William Heaney	1719

A memorial of a deed poll bearing the date second day of January one thousand seven hundred and nineteen made by John Lahy of Aughakilmore in the County of Cavan Gentleman whereby the said John Lahy did for and in consideration of natural love and affection unto his only son William Lahy grant, bargain, sell remise release and confirm unto the said William Lahy all that the said John Lahy's part or proportion of the town and lands of Lower Aughakilmore as the same is set out and distinguished containing sixty six acres be the same more or less situated in the barony of Clonmahon and county of Cavan to hold onto the said William Lahy and the heirs males of his body lawfully begotten the said John Lahy decease and the said deed further reciting that there is justly due and unpaid from the said John Lahy to William Henry of Jinway in the county of Cavan the sum of thirty pounds Ster. which the said John Lahy promised and engaged to pay the said William Henry as part of the marriage portion of Mary Henry als Lahy daughter of the said John Lahy it is therefore the true intent and meaning of the said deed and the so John Lahy did thereby declare that in case the said William Lahy his said son shall dye without issue male of his body lawfully begotten and in consideration of the natural love and affection which the said John Lahy beareth onto the said William Henry his son in law and his said wife Mary Henry als Lahy the said John Lahy's daughter and their issue and for and in consideration of the sum of five shillings Ster. by the so William Henry in hand paid to the said John Lahy before the xxfection of the said deed the receipt whereof is acknowledged. He the said John Lahy did grant bargain sell remise release and for ever confirm unto the said William Henry his heirs and aligns all that the said John Lahy's said part and proportion of the said town lands of Aughakilmore containing sixty six acres be the same more less as the same is now in the possession of the said John Lahy as his own estate in Fee simple absolute and set out and distinguished. Situated Lyeing and being in the barony of clonmahon and county of Cavan afore to hold unto the said William Henry his heirs and aligns for ever together with the reversion and reversions remain same and remainders rents issues and profits of all and singular the premises after the decease of the said John Lahy and William Lahy his son without xxxmale of the said William Lahy's body lawfully begotten as forones which said deed is witnessed by Thomas Heany of upper castletown in the county of west meath. Gent John Lahy of Upper Aughakilmore in the county of cavan xxxx and Hugh Flanagan of Mill Castle in the said county of west meath xxxx and the so Memorial witnessed by the so Thomas Heany and Phil Reilly of the Dublin Gent.

The above Memorial was duly signed and sealed by the above named William Henry in the presence of
- Thomas Heany
- Phil Reilly

The above named Thomas Heany maketh oath that he is a subserving Hipref to the above mentioned deed whereof the above writing is a memorial and also to the said memorial and saw the said deed duely executed by the above named John Lahy and also saw the above named William Henry sign and seal the said Memorial and that the said deed memorial was delivered to Mr William Barry deputy register on the 28th day of May 1736 at or near twelve o clock at noon.

28th Day May 1736 William Parry Dep Reg

Memorial No	From	To	Date
63769	Dillon Collard	Sarah Sizers	1730

A memorial deed of lease bearing the date 2nd day of October, one thousand seven hundred and thirty between Dillon Collard of Castlepollard in the County of Westmeath Esq of the one part and Sarah Sizers alias Lahy and Oliver Sizers of the County of Cavan of the other part. Whereby the said Dillon Collard demised unto the said Sarah Sizers alias Lahy and Oliver Sizers all that part and town and lands of Kilgolagh lying and being in the County of Cavan in as full and ample manner as the said Sarah Sizers now enjoys the same with the Appurtances thereonto belonging To have and to hold the said demised premeses unto the said sarah Sizers and Oliver Sizers their heirs and assigns from the first day of May next during the term of thirty one years yielding and paying thereout yearly and every years during the said term unto the said Dillon Pollard his executor administrators or assigns the yearly rent of Seventy five pounds Ster Crown rent accepted to be paid at two gales Tithe on the first day of November and first day of May the first payment to become due and payable the first day of May next with other usual clauses and covenants the witnesses to the said deed are Richard Woods of Pottleboy John Woods and Oliver Woods both of Aughakilmore in the County of Cavan Gents, and this Memorial is witnessed by the said John Woods and Thomas Lahy of Aughakilmore in the County of Cavan, Gent,

Memorial No	From	To	Date
63539	Pritchard	Haughton	1738

A memorial; of a working declaration of trust dated the tenth day of May, One thousand seven hundred and thirty eight Whereby Even Pritchard did declare that a bill filed by him on the ninth day of May instantiated in the High Court of Chancery against John Fitzgerald Richard Ryland & Sev other sons for the recovery of the lands of Williamstown in County Waterford was filed in frith and further xxx and benefit of Thomas Haughton Esq which said writings as well as this memorial are witnessed by John Lahey & John Meagher of the City of Dublin , Gent.

Evan Richard

John Lahey

Memorial No	From	To	Date
55583	John Laughee, Henry Laughee and Thomas Laughee	Rev Dive Downs	1735

A memorial lease and release dated the thirtieth day of December one thousand seven hundred and thirty four whereby John Laughee, Henry Laughee and Thomas Laughee all of Upper Aghakilmore in the county of Cavan Gent in consideration of one hundred pounds did grant align release and confirm unto the Rev Dive Downs of Cavattown in the county of Meath the all that and whole the fifty four acres of profitable land plantation measure lying in Upper Aghakilmore and also eleven acres one flood profitable land plantation measure lying in the lands of Lavagh then in the possession of the John, Henry and Thomas, being three fourth parts of the estate of Thomas Laughee Deced. In the lands situated in the barony of Clonmahon and county of Cavan to hold for ever subject to rediscon av therin mentioned which said deeds are witnessed by Alex Reilly of Ballinink Gent, James Sinclaire Merch and Thomas Lanktree fletmaker both of oldcastle and all in the county of Meath. And this memorial is witnessed by the said Thomas Lanktree and Edward Fitzgerald of Castletown a for'd Gent Signed and sealed in the presence of (Signatures)

Thomas Lanktree
Edward Fitzgerald.

Thus:

Thomas Lahy 4 Sons:
- *John*
- *Henry*
- *Thomas*
- *William (See 57842 – Fitzpatrick to Lahy)*

Memorial No	From	To	Date
174157	John and Susanna Lahy	Pat Brady	1767

This indenture made the fifth day of December in the year----------
Between William Lahy of Lavagh in the County of Cavan, Gent of the first part [Patrick] Brady of the city of Dublin of the second part, John Lahy of Aughakilmore ----------
Lower [Gent ?] of the third part and Richard Parsons Gent of the said city, of the forth

part. Witness that the said William Lahy for and in consideration of the sum of ten shillings sterling to him in hand paid by the said Patrick Brady at or before the ------------ -- sealing and delivery of these presents the receipts whereof is hereby acknowledged HATH granted bargained sold aligned released and confirmed and by these presents doth grant bargain sell release and confirm unto the said Patrick Brady in his actual possession being by virtue of a deed of bargain release to him thereof made by the said William Lahy for one whole year by indenture bearing date the -- day next before the day of the date of these presents and by force of the statute for transferring uses into posession and to his heirs ALL that and those the thirty five acres in the lands of Aughakilmore Lower, now in the tenure and occupation of the said John Lahy and his mother Susanna Lahy, be the same more or less with all ways waters, water houses, loughs, rivers, bogs, turfbarys, woods, underwoods, timber and timer trees, gardens, orchards, meadows, commons, pastures, feedings mines minerals quarries, royalties and all privileges and appendences and or app-----ances to the said granted premises belonging or in any wise appertaining or with them or any part of them at any time usually occupied possessed or enjoyed all which said granted premises are situate lying and being in the county of Cavan. Aforesaid and the revision and reversions remainder and remain ---- and other rents issues and profits of the said premeses and do every part and parcel thereof and all the Estate, right, Title Interest property profit claim and demand whatsoever both at law in Equity of him the said William Lahy of in and to the said premises and every part thereof TO HAVE AND TO HOLD all and fingul the said lands and premises with all and every the rights meadows and appurtences unto the said Patrick Brady his heirs assigns for and during the term of his natural life to t he use and behoof of the said Patrick Brady and his assigns for and during the term of his natural lifeTo the intent and purpose that the said Patrick Brady by virtue of these presents and of a late act of parliament made in the Kingdom maybe the perfect tenant to the freehold of all and singular the s----remes against whom a good and perfect common recovery may be had and obtained of all ---- the said premises and for that end and purpose it is covernanted and concluded and agreed by and between the said partys and their respective heirs and aligns that the said William Lahy shall forthwith .... Sue forth and -------- or one rights of entry sur Difseisinble post returnable before the justices of his majestys court of common pleasure ------------- herein the said Richard Parsons shall be demanded the said Patrick Brady tenant and the said William Lahy........shall be Vouchee on which writt or writts such proceedings shall be had so as that one or more good and perfect common recovery or recovery according to the usual course of common recoverys shall and may be had and executed of all and singularly ther said lands and premises AND it is hereby declared by and between all the partys to these presents and it is their true intent and meaning that the use of the said recovery or Recoverys so to be had as aforesaid shall be and that the Demandant or Recoverer in the Recovery shall stand seized of the said lands and premises with their Appurtances. To the use of and behoof of the said John Lahy his heirs aligns for ever and to and for -- other use intent or purpose whatsoever in Witness Whereof the partys aforesaid have hereonto put their hands and seals the day and year first here written

Memorial No	From	To	Date
Salt Lake City – Family History Centre Film# 596411 T, Box & Order# 2915 of 2943 Pg 276 of 301	276 Prerogative Case Paper 1769		1769

Citation on the part of Acheson against Lahy. Margaret Lahy and James Lahy the executors named in the last will of Thomas Lahy late of Aughakilmore in the county of Cavan, deceased – to appear before us – In the house of the Rt Hon Philip Tisdall Esq situate in Leinster, Dublin on 11 April next – To deposit in the registry of this court the said will and accept or refuse the brother of the executor thereof together with administration of all singles the goods etc of said deceased otherwise to his cause why letters of Adm of said deceased with the will amended should not be granted with Robert Acheson of the city of Dublin by financial seal of set deceased.

3 March 1769

Whereas there issued a citation against Margaret Lahy and James Lahy the executors named in the will of Thomas Lahy late of Aughakilmore Upper, Co Cavan, deceased. And whereas said citation was expected returned returned and whereas said Margaret Lahy and James Lahy the impungants in the above cited case have neglected to introduce said original will of said Thomas Lahy dead – Philip Tindall Esq Doctor of Laws – further proceeding in said business did at the petition of the proctor of said Robert Acheson decree a citation to issue against said Margaret Lahy and James Lahy in this case why they shall not be exonerated for their manifest contempt in not appearing.

Said Margaret and James Lahy to appear before us on 4th Nov next – there to show cause why should not be exonerated for their manifest contempt in not appearing at the time and place specified (and their effects) in said citation

14 July 1769

Memorial No	From	To	Date
22030	Thomas & Margaret Lahy	Booth	1779

A memorial of articles of a release made this ninth day of July in the year of our lord one thousand seven hundred and seventy nine whereas Thomas Lahy and Margaret Lahy of Aghakilmore in the county of Cavan [renused] released and forever discharged Elinor Booth (otherwise Lahy) and John Lahy her son both of Williamstown in the county of

Westmeath, their heirs, Execs and aligns from all manner of actions, suits, debts, dues and sums of money accounts [rec___] bonds, bills, wills and specialty covenants contracts, [compromises], agreements, promises, [convaces] judgements, extents claims and demands whatsoever in law and Equity against said Elinor Booth or John Lahy from the beginning of the world to the date of these presents when said release is witnessed by Francis Lahy of Ballina and George McTavern of Tullakelen, both of the county of Cavan and this memorial is also witnessed by the said George McTavern and [Byron Corry] of the city of Dublin. William O'Reilly also witness.

Analysis

1. Thomas and Margaret of Aghakilmore – assumed husband and wife
2. Daughter Elinor – married a Booth *(William Booth in 1757)*
3. John and Elinor released from all deeds etc
4. Francis Lahy of Ballina = close relation

Memorial No	From	To	Date
222029	Thomas and Wife Margaret	John Lahy of Williamstown	1779

A memorial of the intended articles of agreement made between Thomas Lahy of Lower Aughakilmore in the county of Cavan of the one part and John Lahy of Williamstown in the county of Westmeath of the other part and Margaret wife of the said Thomas Lahy of the third part the thirteenth day of December one thousand seven hundred and seventy nine reciting that the said Thomas Lahy was seized and possessed of an estate of inheritance in the town and lands of Aughakilmore Upper, now in the tenure of Thomas Heney and Lower Aughakilmore in the possession of John Masterson, Henry Lahy and the said Thomas Lahy containing sixty acres be the same more or less and further reciting that the said Thomas Lahy in consideration of five shillings xx to him in hand paid by the said John Lahy, he the said Thomas Lahy did grant bargain sell and make over onto the said John Lahy all and singular the aforesaid lands and premesis of Upper and Lower Aughakilmore and all the said Thomas Lahy's right and title therein after mention that is to say in trust to permit the said Thomas Lahy and his assigns to receive the rents and profits of said premesis during his life and after his death in case said Margaret his wife shall in consideration to permit his or her assigns to receive of said premesis a third of all the real and personal estate which the said Thomas Lahy shall die possessed of and the remainder to the use and benefit of said Thomas Lahys heirs lawfully begotten of the body of the said Margaret for ever nevertheless to suffer said Thomas Lahy to charge the premesis with such sums of money that appears to be lawful in firstly due or may be lived by the reasonable request (and that said Thomas Lahy is not to sell or Mortgage any part of said premesis without the consent of the said John Lahy) of the the said John Lahy and that from a will there under his hand and seal which said article contains several other clauses and consents and is witnessed by William Lahy of Aughakilmore in the said county of Cavan and George McFarren of Ballahelen in the said county and this memorial is also witnessed by said George McFarren and Bryan Corry of the city of Dublin.

Memorial No	From	To	Date
National Library of Ireland	Francis Lahy	Borrows	1779

This indenture made the fifth xxxx day of November in the year of our lord one thousand seven hundred and seventy nine between Francis Lahy eldest son and heir at law of James Lahy of Upper Aughakilmore in the county of Cavan, Gent of the first part, Rebecca Burrowes of Killiconan in the county of Cavan Oferes Esq of the second part, the said James Lahy father of the said Francis of the third part and Alexander Burrowes of Cavan in the said county of Cavan and John Lahy of Williamstown in the county of Westmeath, Gent of the fourth, whereas a marriage is shortly intended to be had and solemised between the said Francis Lahy and the said Rebecca Burrowes and whereas the said James Lahy is now seized and possessed of the several denominations of land herein after mentioned by deed bearing date the second day of July one thousand six hundred and sixty seven, and made by Thos. Coote late of Cootehill in the county of Cavan Esg. Deceased to Patrick Lahy deceased at the yearly rent of one peppercorn in consideration of the sum of sixty pounds sterl. That is to say sixty acres or thereabouts in the townland of Upper Aughakilmore as the same is now possessed by the said James Lahy or his under tenants, whereas said land and premesis are situate lying and being in the Barony of Clonmahon and County of Cavan aforesaid and whereas the said James Lahy is also seized and possessed of a part of the townland of Lavagh, situate also in the Barony of Clonmahon and county of Cavan aforesaid low. This indenture witnesseth that in consideration of the said intended marriage portion of the said Rebecca being two hundred pounds , and also in consideration of five shillings ster. to him the said James Lahy in hand paid before the ensealing and delivery of these presents the xxuipt whereof he the said James Lahy both hereby acknowledge and for divers other good causes and consideration, him thereunto moving he the said James Lahy hath granted bargained sold released and confirmed and by these presents doth grant bargain sell release and confirm unto the said Alexander Burrowes and John Lahy in their actual profession now being by deed bearing date the day next before the day of the date of these presents and by force of the statute for transferring for transferring uses into professions and to their heirs all that those the several denominations of land herein before particularly mint except as herein after is excepted. With all and xxx singular their rights members and apprentances to have and to hold the said lands and premesis herein before anointed or intended to be _____ release with their and _y of their xxx rights. John Lahy and their heirs to and for the several uses intents and purposes whatsoever that is to say to the use and behoof of the said Alexander Burrowes and John Lahy and their heirs upon first only for preserving the contingent and estates herein mentioned and his further covenant and agreed upon by and between the said James Lahy and the said Francis Lahy that the said James Lahy shall and will on the day after the Marriage of the said Francis give up and surrender unto the said Francis Lahy or his aligns the lives and peaceable profession that part of the said lands of Upper Aughakilmore which is now possessed by the said James his under tenants or assigns and the said James Lahy both hereby for him his executors and administrators covenant and agree to and with the said Francis Lahy his execs and assigns to give up and surrender to the Francis his execors, admins or assigns on the first day of May next the ___ and peaceable profession of the dwelling house wherein the said James now lives on the said lands of Upper Aughakilmore together will all and singular the offices and other appointances there__ belonging in the same repair and condition in which they now are and the said James Lahy doth for him, his execs, admins and assigns covenant promise grant and agree to and with the said Francis Lahy his execs admin and assigns in manner form and following that is to say that from and immediately after the decease of the said James Lahy, he the said Francis Lahy his execos, Admins and Assigns that stand seized and possessed and be installed unto all that part of the townland of Lavagh aforesaid with its apprentances which is now possessed by the said James Lahy his under tenants or assigns subject to ten pounds per annum jointure for Hannah Lahy wife of the said James in case she shall survive the said James her present husband and also to eight pounds yearly as a jointure for Margaret Groves, widow of Thomas Lahy deceased and four hundred pounds for the younger children of the said James Lahy and in case any of the the said younger children of the said James Lahy shall happen to die before he or she shall attain their age twenty one years or day of marriage, then and in such case the part or proportion of such child or children shall so happen to die shall go to be divided amongst the survivor or survivors of the said children share and share alike. And it is also covenanted and agreed upon by and between there parties to these presents that if it shall happen that the said Francis Lahy shall die without issue of his body lawfully begotten on the body of the said Rebecca that then and in such case the lands and premises hereby settled upon the said Francis Lahy shall ___ and go to the next lawfull heir of the Lahy family subject nevertheless to the above encumbrances and chargeable with four hundred pounds for the younger children of the said Francis and also chargeable with any sum ___ not exceeding one hundred pounds when the said Francis is hereby empowered to charge or encumber the said lands with in case he the said Francis shall think proper so to do and in case the said Francis shall happen to die before the said Rebecca his intended wife then and in such case all the lands and premises hereby settled or intended to be settled that stand charged and chargeable with an annunity or yearly rent charge of twenty pounds Ster. as and for the jointure of the said Rebecca which said sum of twenty pounds Ster. shall be paid and payable to the said or her aligns by two equal and even gates in every year, the first payment thereof to be made to the said Rebecca or her aligns on the first day of May or the first day of November , whichever shall first happen after the decease of the said Francis Lahy with full power to the said Rebecca and her aligns during her natural life to disbrain lease for and recover the same of all and singular the said lands and premesis hereby granted or settled and the said James Lahy doth hereby covenant promise and agree to and with the parties to these presents that the said lands tenants and premises hereby granted or settled or intended to be granted or settled and every part thereof with all and singular their apprentices now are and from henceforth shall continue to remain and be unto the said Francis Lahy his heirs and aligns free and clear and freely and clearly acquitted exonerated and discharged of and from all manner of former and other bargains, sales, gifts, grants, jointures, doweries, judgements, executions or any manner of encumbances whatsoever had made committed or done or caused to lie had made committed or done by the said James Lahy or any other person or persons whatsoever and that the said Francis Lahy his heirs and aligns and every of them shall or lawfully may from time to time and at all times hereafter have, hold, use, occupy or ___ and enjoy all and singular the said lands and tenants hereby granted and every part and ____ therof with all and singular their and every of their apprentices and all and every the ____ issues and profits thereof except as ___ excepted without any manner of the said trouble, eviction or molestation whatsoever or by the said James Lahy, his executors _____ person or persons whatsoever lawfully claiming or to claim by from and under him them or any of them _____ to a duplicate hereof let their hands and affixed their seals.

A True Copy of
Francis Lahy
Marriage Settlement

Witnessed by James Sheridan

Memorial No	From	To	Date
202256	John Lahy	Freeman Wilton	1785

To the register appointed by act of parliament for registering deeds settlements in Ireland

A memorial of an intended deed or settlement of marriage bearing date the thirteenth day of december one thousand seven hundred and eighty five between John Lahy of Aughakilmore and Elizabeth his wife and Patrick Lahy son of the said John Lahy of the one part and Freeman Wilton and Elizabeth Wilton his daughter of the other part both of Derryn all in the county of Cavan reciting that a marriage was intended to be had solemized between the said Patrick Lahy and Elizabeth Wilton and that the said John Lahy stands seized in Fee of forty acres of the said town and lands of Aughakilmore situate in said county of Cavan. They the [said] John Lahy and his wife Elizabeth did for the consideration of said marriage and of the marriage portion of said deed must grant assign convey and settle upon the said Patrick Lahy during his life one half of lands of Aughakilmore with remainder to the eldest son of said marriage and to his heirs male forever with a jointure on Elizabeth his said intended wife in case she should survive the said PAtrick Lahy to be paid on the days and the times in said deed is [mentioned] with liberty to [Distrain ?] for same in case of nonpayment which said deed is witnessed by John Heogan, Henry Maxwell William Wade and John Lahy and this memorial is also witnessed by the said John Keogan and Chris Bredin of [Richill] in said County.

Freeman Wilton

The above named John Keogan maketh oath that he saw the above named John Lahy, Freeman Wilton, Patrick Lahy and Elizabeth Wilton duely seal and execute the above recited deed whereof the above writing is a memorial and also saw the said Freeman Wilton sign and seal the said Memorial and sayth that this depos[ition] is a subscribing witness to the said deed and memorial

John Keoghan

Sworn before me and my sergeant at Cavan in the county of Cavan the 26th Day of Aprin 1791.

Lahy & Wife to Lahy

Memorial No	From	To	Date
250839	James Lahy	George Kerr	1786

A memorial of an intended deed bearing the date the thirteenth day of April one thousand seven hundred and eighty six made between James Lahy of Lavagh and Francis Lahy of [Killconnele] in the county of Cavan, gent of the one part and George Kerr of Finea in the county of Westmeath gent of the other part reciting that the said James and Francis Lahy did by inherited deed of lease bearing date the twenty seventh day of April one thousand seven hundred and eighty four demise onto the said George Kerr all that and those that part of the town and lands of Lavagh now in the possession of the representations of Thomas Cheevers deceased or his under tenants containing sixteen acres or thereabouts. Also all that part of the town and lands of Lavagh [afews] now in the possession of George [McDarren] or his undertenants containing eight acres or thereabouts. Also all that part of the town and lands in the possession of James Lahy or his undertenants containing forty two acres or thereabouts said lands situated in the county of Cavan aforesaid to hold said George Kerr his Execs advisors from the first days of May this next for the term of thirty one years subject to the yearly rent in said lease reserved said deed whereof this is a memorial witnessed that the said George Kerr there in consideration ___ month surrender and give up unto the said James and Francis Lahy all his right title and interest of his to the demised ___ to the said James and Francis Lahy their heirs and aligns for the rest [residue] and consideration of the term And the said James and Francis Lahy did hereby accept of the surrender of the lease audited and released the ___ Kerr his heirs _____ from all rent and arrears of rent due or to out of demise by virtue of lease which said deed was witnessed by Andrew Bell of the city of Dublin and James Buits of Granard in the county of Longford, gent and this memorial is witnessed by James Buch and Elizabeth Kerr of Finea in the county of Westmeath.

Analysis

James and Francis were brothers – and inherited land in 1784 – father died around then

Location of Killconnele ? Possibly Kilconny in north Cavan ?

Memorial No	From	To	Date

300648	Richard Lahy	Henry Maxwell	1793

A memorial of an intended deed made the fifteenth day of July one thousand seven hundred and ninety three between Richard Lahy of Aghakilmore in the county of Cavan , gentleman of the one part and Henry Maxwell of Crover in the said county of Cavan gentleman of the other part whereby after reciting several judgements had by the said Henry Maxwell against the said Richard Lahy and several deeds and writings therefore had between them , he the said Richard Lahy did for him his heirs, executors, administrators for and in consideration of the sum of four hundred and seventy nine pounds therein mentioned to have been paid [set] sell transfer, convey and assign all the town and lands of Aghakilmore in the county of Cavan aforesaid commonly pronounced or called the Cross to hold to him the said Henry Maxwell his heirs, executors, administrators and aligns for ever (together with all his right and tithe therein) subject however to the provision or condition of redemption therein particularly set out and mentioned as by said deed may ____ fully appear and said deed also contains covenants on the part of the said Richard Lahy his heirs and aligns to pay the sum of four hundred and seventy nine pounds sterling with lawfull interest and costs and that he had in himself sufficient power to make such deed in the manner and form thereof and would at any time or times thereafter make do and execute any other deed or deeds to collaborate said deed as should be deemed necessary or expedient and it also contains a covenant irrevocably for the said Henry Maxwell, his heirs, executors administrators and aligns to [ash] take [perceive] receive [_ice] for and recover in his or their own name or names the yearly sum or annuity of twenty eight pounds fifteen shillings sterling until the said sum of four hundred and seventy nine pounds sterling together with with all interest and costs that shall or should arise or grow [_ice] thereon should be fully paid off discharged contented and satisfied and said deed also gives the said Henry Maxwell a power to enter upon any part of the said lands of Agakilmore or any other lands which the said Richard Lahy his heirs or aligns shall be possessed of or intitled unto in right of him the said Richard Lahy and [distain] the same and dispose of the [dishefs] according to law for the said annuity of twenty eight pounds fifteen shillings sterling or any arrears thereof until the said sum of four hundred and seventy nine pouinds sterling and the interest and costs should be paid off as aforesaid which said deed and this memorial are witnessed by Robert Coyle of the city of Dublin, gentleman attourney and James Lord of Fortland in the county of Cavan, gentleman.

Analysis
_____

1. Judgements were made by Henry Maxwell against Richard Lahy (for what ?)
2. had to surrender 'The Cross' until £479 paid off at the rate of £28 per year
3. Refers to earlier deeds / writings
4. 1st mention of 'The Cross' at Aughakilmore
5. Another deed 348967 dated 1800 details lands in Aghakilmore to the 'late Henry Maxwell – for amount of £1465 !!
6. Richard got married a year earlier – to Elizabeth Thornton (deed 294154)

Memorial No	From	To	Date
332001	Thomas Lahy	Terence Joey	1797

A memorial of deed poll or lease bearing the date the eighteenth day of October in the year of our lord one thousand seven hundred and ninety seven made between Thomas Lahy of Aghakilmore in the county of Cavan, Gent of the one part and Terence Joey of Aghakilmore aforesaid publican,. Reciting that the said Thomas Lahy for and in consideration of the yearly rents and covenants hath demised granted sold and to farm ___ unto the said Terence Joey all that parts of the lands of Aghakilmore aforesaid containing ten acres with the houses, Edifes and buildings therein to belonging for and during the term time and space of the natural life of the said Thomas Lahy or forty one years, whichever shall last longest at the yearly rent of one pound eight shillings and three half pence, that for every acre the same shall [contain] together with the bog and all the [Appuntenansees] therein to belonging and said deed contains clauses and covenants may more fully [appear] and said deed is witnessed by Andrew O'Reilly of [Lefsanny] gent and common [leapry] of Pottlebog, farmer and this memorial is also witnessed by the said [Andrew] O'Reilly and Bryan O'Reilly of [Lefsanny] aforesaid gent.

Analysis

Thomas rented 10 acres of Lower Aghakilmore to Terence Joey – a publican. Could this be the start of the 'Cross' Public house (which exists on a plot of about 10 acres).

Memorial No	From	To	Date
516851	Patrick Lahy	John Lahy	1821

A memorial of a marriage article of indenture of four parts bearing the date the twenty sixth day of January One thousand eight hundred and twenty one between Patrick Lahy of Drumeeny in the county of Cavan Gentleman of the first part, John Lahy of the same (son of the said Patrick Lahy) of the second part, Harriett Strong daughter of William Strong of Kilnahard in the said county of Cavan Spinster of the third part and James Strong of Tawlaught in the said county of Cavan, Gentleman of the fourth part.

Whereas a marriage is intended shortly to be had and solomised between the said John Lahy and Harriett Strong. Now this indenture witnesseth that for and consideration of the said intended marriage of the marriage portion of the said Harriett Strong in the case the same shall take effect and in consideration of the sum of three hundred pounds sterling the marriage portion of the said Harriett Strong to the said Patrick Lahy in hand at and before the sealing and perfection of those presents and also in consideration of the natural love and affection of the said Patrick Lahy for his said son
John Lahy and for making a provision for the use of the said Harriet Strong and the issue of said marriage and for aligning and afsurfing the lands and premises herin after mentioned upon the trusts and for the purposes houn after mentioned and declared concerning the same and the sum of ten shillings by the said James Strong to the said Patrick Lahy in hand paid after before the sealing and delivery of these presents will and

truly paid the receipt whereby is hereby acknowledged that the said Patrick Lahy hath bargained sold aligned transferred and set over unto the said James Strong and by these presents doth bargain sell align transfer and set over unto the said James Strong in his actual possession now living by virtue of a bargain viable to him thereof made by the said Patrick Lahy for five shillings consideration xxxxx by indenture bearing date the day next before the date of these presents for one whole year commencing from the day next before the day of the date of these presents and by force of the stature for transferring uses into possession and to his heirs and aligns forever all that those the town and lands of Aughakilmore situate in the county of Cavan aforesaid to have and to hold the said lands and premises hereby alighned or intended so to be with the appurtinanus onto the said James Strong his heirs and aligns forever upon trust nevertheless and to and for such intents and purposes as hereafter mentioned expressed and declared concerning the same that is to say in trust for the said Patrick Lahy his heirs until the solemising of the said marriage and from and after the solemisation of the said marriage the upon trust that the said James Strong his heirs and aligns and shall during the lives of the said John Lahy and Harriett Strong his intended wife permit the said John Lahy to have and receive the Rents issues and Profits of one half of the said lands during the life of the said Patrick Lahy and from and after his will to permit and suffer the said John Lahy upon trust and to permit and suffer the said Harriett Strong and her aligns if she shall survive the said John Lahy her intended husband to receive and the sum of twenty pounds sterling per annum as a provision and jainter during her life in Leiw Bar and satisfaction of her power or thirds which she can or may claim out of the said lands and premesis or wherin the said John Lahy is or at any time hereafter shall be xxxx the said sum of twenty pounds sterling to be issuing and payable out of one half of the said lands and premises during the life of the said Patrick Lahy for in and after his xxxx to receive and take the said sum of twenty pounds sterling per annum out of the rent and profits of the whole of said lands during her life xxxx life to the sum of four hundred pounds sterling as a provision for the younger children of said marriage with power nevertheless to the said John Lahy during his life to dispose of the said sum of four hundred pounds during his life then and in such case that the said Harriett Strong shall by died or will direct or appoint and in case he shall make no such disposal of the said sum of four hundred pounds during his life then and in such case the said Harriett Strong shall by died or will dispose of the same to such younger child or children as she may by deed or will direct or appoint and moreover that the said Patrick Lahy and John Lahy their heirs or Admrs and all other person or persons having or claiming any estate right take trust or interest of in and to said lands and premises or any part thereof or in trust for them shall and will at any times hereafter upon the request of the said James Strong best set the proper costs and charges of the said John Lahy his heirs or aligns make and execute or cause to be done and executed all such further and other lawfull acts conveyances and assurances in law whatsoever required for the further and latter assuring and surviving the said xxxx and which indenture is witnessed by Christopher Robinson and John Brady.

Memorial No	From	To	Date
560028	John Packenham	Ann Stratford	1828

	Leahy		

A memorial of a deed of marriage settlement made between John Peckenham Lahy gentleman of the one part and Anne Stratford widow and xxxx, executor of Robert Stratford late of annesgrove otherwise mannea of the second part and Anne stratford spinster daughter of the said deceased of the third part enlied into and concluded the eleventh day of February one thousand eight hundred and twenty eight.

Whereby after reciting that in consideration of a marriage intended to be had and solemized between the said John Packenham Lahy was to receive the sum of eight hundred pounds late Irish currency with other the several claims to which he might be entitled pursuient to the last will of the said Robert Stratford bearing the date the twentieth day of January one thousand eight hundred and twenty five and also for selling a competent jointure and maintenance on the said Anne Stratford the intended bride during her natural life. The said deed witnessed that in consideration of the said John Packenham Lahy did thirley for himself and his heirs, executors, administrators and assigns declare it to be the intent and meaning thereof that in case she the said Anne Stratford his intended wife should outlive him thre said John Packenham Lahy without lawful xxx and remain his widow unmarried she should receive and recover from and off the lands of Capragh and Mote both in the county of Cavan, the annunity or yearly sum of one hundred pounds sterling to be paid her in five even and equal payments as the rents xxx and profits should or might become live and payable thereout and provided th said Anne Stratford the intended wife of the said John Packenham Lahy should have issue and out live him as aforesaid then and in such case her yearly annunity should only be forty pounds payable out of the lands of Caprah and Mote as aforesaid in equal payments in manner aforesaid and that all and every property which the said John Packenham Lahy should or would thereafter accumulate should be subject and liable to the payment thereof and by which said deed of which this is a memorial xx the said John Packenham Lahy for the further consideration of five shillings to him paid by the said Anne Stratford widow and Anne Atratford spinster her said daughter the intended wife of the said John Packenham Lahy, he the said John Packenham Lahy granted and confirmed all the said lands of Capragh and Mote and all other property he should thereafter be possessive of either in fee, simple fee xxx or copy hold and that freely and clearly discharged of and from all debts dues judgements extents, executions or other incumbances to hold unto the said Anne Stratford widow in trust for the sole and separate use and benefit of the said Anne stratford the daughter of the said deceased and the intended wife of the said John Packenham Lahy to and after payment of the said annuity or yearly sum of one hundred pounds or forty pounds as the case might be with power to distain in case of non-payment thereof and which deed also contains a covenant for further assurance and was duely signed sealed and delivered by the said John Packenham Lahy, Anne Stratford and Anne Stratford and witnessed by Patrick Lahy of Drumeeny in the county of Cavan, gentlemen and Mich Byrne of Annesgrove otherwise Mannann in the county of Westmeath xxx clerk and this memorial is xxx signed and sealed by the said John Packenham Lahy and witnessed by the said Patrick Lahy and Mich Byrne.

John P. Lahy

Patt Lahy

Memorial No	From	To	Date
155	Susanna Lahy		1831

A memorial of the intended articles of Agreement made entered into and concluded upon by and between Susanna Lahy of Capprah in the county of Cavan widow of Henry Lahy of Capprah aforesaid deceased of the first part, John Lahy of Upper Aghakilmore in the said county of Upper Aghakilmore in the said county of Cavan, Gent of the second part, which said John is eldest son and heir at law of Henry Lahy, George Lahy gent of Capprah in the said county of Cavan of the third part, William Lahy of Capprah aforesaid gent of the fourth part, Henry Lahy of Clonloghan also in the said county of Cavan of the fifth part, Robert Strong of Capprah of the said county of Cavan gent of the sixth part, James Lahy and Anne Lahy both of Capprah aforesaid of the seventh part. Whereas the said Henry Lahy junior was in and prior to the sixth of January one thousand eight hundred and thirty one seized in fee of the town and lands of Upper and Lower Aghakilmore and Capprah and was also possessed of a variety of cattle property including household furniture ----- and the said Henry Lahy by his last will and testament duly executed to pass freehold estates did demise and bequeath unto his testators eldest son John Lahy ----- all that and those the lands of Upper and Lower Aghakilmore for the term of his natural life with remainder upon his testators to his son Henry Lahy and his and lease but subject to the payment by the said Henry of twenty pounds sterling to each of the children which might be item of the said John and the said testator so gave and bequeathed said lands ---- to the payment of several parties having and claiming interests under said will and the said George Lahy and William who are entitled to the lands of Capprah by virtue of a deed of conveyance from their said father hence came to an agreement and settlement of their rights and claims under said will or otherwise to the property of their said father in order to prevent trouble or litigation and that from hence forth the said several portions in consideration shall have and hold, take and receive persons and accept the several lure ? of Henry or yearly protments herin after provided for and received in full and satisfaction of their claims under said will or otherwise. Now these presents witness that in assurance of the said agreement and for and in consideration of a release of all claims or right to ____ or thirds of common lands or under said will or otherwise to which the said Susanna Lahy is in any manner entitled to and for and in consideration of ten shillings to him paid at or before the unsealing and delivery of these presents, the said John Lahy doth given granted, sold assigned and made over and by these presents doth give, grant, leave, assign and make over unto the said Susaanna Lahy and her assigns during the term of her natural life and annuity or yearly rent charged of nine pounds to be ------- and payable out of all that and those the said lands of Aghakilmore Upper and Lower the said annuity be paid and payable and to commence and begin on the first day of May one thousand eight hundred and thirty one and to be made by two equal half yearly payments or portions on every first day of May and first day of November in every year as aforesaid and if the said half yearly payments shall be delayed or held back for the space of twenty one days after the payment to be made it shall be lawful to and for the said Susanna Lahy or her assigns unto the said to enter and disfrain in such a manner as is ---- between landlord and tenent and the property she to dispose of according to law until the said annuity be fully paid satisfied and discharged and the said John Lahy for the councel aforesaid of a full release and discharged of the said James Lahy, Anne Lahy, Robert Strong and Harriet his wife of their claims under said will to the several legacies bequeathed to them in consideration of five shillings a piece by them to the said John Lahy doth hereby covenant promise and agree for him self his heirs, Executors, and assigns in manner following that is to say that he and they shall and will and twenty pay or cause to be paid unto the said James Lahy on the first day of November in the year one thousand eight hundred and thirty five with careful interest for the same the just and full sum of sixty pounds sterling and that the said John Lahy his heirs, Executors and administrators shall pay or cause to be paid unto the said Anne Lahy upon the day of her marriage and the just and all sum of twenty five pounds sterling in twelve months after the said marriage in twelve months after her said marriage provided the said James and Anne Lahy act agreeable to the wish of their mother and Uncle George Strong. And he the said John Lahy his executors and assigns and aligns shall will and timely pay or cause to be paid unto the said Robert Strong and Harriet Strong the just and full sum of thirty five pounds sterling by annual payments of ten pounds sterling, the first yearly payment to be made on the first day of November next and the said Henry Lahy (party here to) in order to settle all differences that might arise and course of ----- have now deceased to him and for him caused of the sum of ten shillings sterling to him in hand paid by the said John Lahy. He the said Henry Lahy doth grant bargain sell release and confirm unto the said John Lahy his heirs and aligns all tenency or any reversionary or other estate right, letter or inherit of or to the said lands of Upper and Lower Aghakilmore, to hold the same unto the said John Lahy his heirs and assigns for ever and his and their own proper estate and whereas by an indenture therefore made by and between the said Henry Lahy deceased and his sons the said William and George Lahy, he the said Henry Lahy did grant to cause and confirm unto his sons William and George the Lands of Capprah forever. Now these present witness that the said George Lahy doth hereby in consideration of five shillings and for the others consideration before being mentioned will and grant unto the said Susanna Lahy for his natural life the full sum of eight pounds sterling until the marriage of the said Anne Lahy and James Lahy and that from then and from henceforth the said George Lahy shall pay or cause to be paid unto the said Susanna Lahy the sum of five pounds sterling only yearly and every year during the life of the said Susanna, the said sum of five pounds and eight pounds to be paid and payable and charged upon the proportion of the said George Lahy of the said lands of Capprah and the said Susanna to be entitled and she is hereby authorised to ----- the --------- half years in equal portions on every first day of May and first day of November to commence and be payable from the first day of May one thousand eight hundred and thirty one, and the said William Lahy doth covenant for himself his heirs and assigns to furnish give and supply unto the said Susanna Lahy from henceforth until the marriage of the said James Lahy and Anne Lahy yearly and every year one cows grass winter and summer with sufficiency of hay or fodder suck cow to be fed with and in the summer Marr** of any of his own litter ---- And it is by said deed declared and agreed that the said susanna Lahy shall and may quickly and peaceably have hold and enjoy one half of the dwelling house in Capprah and the furniture therein during her natural life without the interference or control of any person whatsoever and that from and after her demise the said George Lahy shall have possession and enjoy the said house and furniture. And the said George Lahy from and after of the said James and Anne Lahy shall graze and feed a cow for his said mother in the same manner as his own. ---- As said agreement is witnessed by Thomas Lahy of Aghakilmore, James Strong and Thomas Donohoe of Tawlaught all in the county of Cavan, farmers, and which deed is dated the seventh day of May one thousand eight hundred and thirty two.

Signed and sealed in the presence of
George Strong   *James Strong*   *George Lahy*

Memorial No	From	To	Date
10	Patrick Lahy	O Reilly	1851

6/12/1848
Patrick Leahy of Derrin and Jane O Reilly of Lislin (Widow) & Thomas Leahy of Drumeeny and John Brady of Lavagh.

Jane O Reilly in possession under the will of her late husband (James O Reilly) – dated 24/2/1847 of 36 acres of lands in Lislin, barony of castleraheran for her natural life under a certain deed made to her late husband James O Reilly by Luke Reilly of Mullagh dated 9/11/1821 reciting that the said Patrick Leahy was seized and possessed of the lands of Derrin containing about 19 acres under a lease from the late Lord Farnham dated 18/3/1834 and that he was also possessed of the lands of Aghaconny in the barony of Clonmahon containing about 45 acres held in fee by him.
A marriage was intended to be had between said Patrick and said Jane O Reilly and that the said properties should be conveyed to the said Thomas Leahy and John Brady as trustees for the uses of said deed mentioned.

For sum of 5s sold and made over to said Thomas Leahy & John Brady:
36 acres in Lislin
19 acres in Derrin (& lives leases therein)
45 acres in Aghaconny.

If Jane survives Patrick she gets £25 year. If she dies before him then Patrick gets all the land from the trustees.

Witnessed by John Sheridan of Bawny & Denis Brady of Lavagh.

Memorial No	From	To	Date
2			1923

A memorial of an indenture of Marriage Settlement bearing the date the 22nd day of August nine hundred and twenty three and made between John Leahy senior of Aughakilmore in the county of Cavan farmer of the first part Julia Leahy of same place wife of the said John Leahy senior of the second part, John Leahy junior of the same place farmer of the third part and Charles McClean of Duffcastle Ballyjamesduff in the County of Cavan farmer of the fourth part whereby after reciting as therin it was witnessed that in consideration of the natural love and affection and of the intended marriage between said John Leahy junior and Anna May McClean and in pursuance of the therin recited Agreement the said John Leahy senior as beneficial owner did thereby grant and convey unto the said Charles McClean all that and those that farm of land situate in the townland of Lower Aughakilmore in the county of Clonmahon and County of Cavan containing twenty seven acres statute measure or thereabouts with the licensed premises shop house and all buildings thereon and appartences there onto belonging to hold the said premises unto the said Charles McClean his heirs executors and administrators in trust for the use of the said John Leahy senior and the said Julia Leahy without impeachment of waste during the joint lives of the said John Leahy senior and Julia Leahy and the survivors of them and upon the death of the survivor of the said John Leahy senior and Julia Leahy then to the said John Leahy junior his heirs and assigns absolutely together with the publican's license and all the cattle horses stock crops farming implements household furniture and stock in trade which might then be thereon or therein And it was witnessed that in further pursuance of the said Agreement and for the considerations aforesaid the said Julia Leahy as Beneficial owner did thereby grant and convey onto the said John Leahy junior his heirs and assigns All that land - that farm of land situate in the townland of Upper Aughakilmore in the Barony of Clonmahon and County of Cavan containing four acres and two roods statute measure or thereabouts with all the buildings thereon and appurtances thereonto belonging to hold the said premises unto and to the use of the said John Leahy junior his heirs and assigns forever and it was also witnessed that in further pursuance of the said Agreement and for the considerations aforesaid the said John Leahy senior as Beneficial owner did thereby assign unto the said John Leahy junior All that and those that farm of land situate in the townland of Clonoose in the barony of Clonmahon and county of Cavan containing forty three acres and two roods and eleven perches statute measure or thereabouts with the houses and buildings thereon and all the appurtances thereonto belonging to hold the said premises unto the said John Leahy junior his executors administrators and assigns for all the tenancy tenant right term estate and interest of the said John Leahy senior therein or thereto subject to the yearly rent payable under and the conditions contained in said Judicial Agreement under which same held and subject to the covenants conditions and agreements therein contained which said Indenture as to the execution thereof by the said John Leahy Senior, Julia Leahy, John Leahy Junior and Charles McClean respectively is witnessed by John R. Halpin solicitor Cavan and Thomas Brady Auctioneer and farmer of Aughakilmore, Ballynarry in the county of Cavan.

5   Notes on Privately Held Deeds

These are a few transcriptions and notes I have made on some Privately held deeds that I've had access to.

	From	To	Date
[Short Version of Deed]	Patrick Laghy of Tawlaght	Thomas Coote	1671
This indenture dated the first day of July the year of our lord God ----------- twentieth xxx year of the reign of out soverign Lord Charles the second by the grace of God of England Scotland and Ireland, King Defender of the faith, Between Thomas Coote of Cootehill in the county of Cavan of the one part and Patrick Laghy of Tawlaght in the county of Cavan gengtleman of the other part. Witness that the said Thomas Coote aforesaid in consideration of the sum of ten shillings ? of lawfull money of England to him in hand payed porfetting hereof by the said Patrick Laghy herin whereof the said Thomas Coote doth hereby acknowledge hath bargained and sold and by he Gents doth bargain and sell ontfo the said Patrick Laghy all the land tenants and -------- hereafter mentioned (that is to say) out of Taughlawt fifteen acres and woods profitable plantation measured out, Out of Akhakilmore seventy two acres profitable lands of like Irish plantation measured out of Moydristan, sixty six acres and woods profitable land plantation measures all for lands and -------- are lying and being in the Barony of Clonmahon and County of Cavan and ------ in the one hundred and fifty acres and woods profitable land and plantation measured to two hundred forty six acres one root English measure. Together with all and singular the houses, Edifices, buildings, woods -------, bogs, mountains, heath, tenemants ---------- commodation ------- and --------- in any way belonging or appointing to have and to hold the -------- mentioned or intended to be bargained and lands and every ------ snd psrt sll thereof with all and every ---------- commodation dadvantage and ------ belonging as to the said Pat Laghy his Exorata -------- and aligns for and during the ---- andsxard of two xxx yearor remmorroring from the day before ------ and from -----forth fully to ------- yelding and paving therfore unto the said Thomas Coote, his heirs and assigns during the said ---- and yearly rent of one xxxxxx found on the first day of November in arth of the said years if the same co lawfully demanded. An witnesse wherof tho said parties to presente into ---------- sell their lands and sealed the day and year first above. R Cognit Coran me 16 Die Novembris 1671 --- Thus 15 Acres Tawlaught 72 Acres Aughakilmore 66 Acres Moydristan 150 Acres Total of 246 Acres		

	From	To	Date
[Long Version of Deed]	Patrick Laghy of Tawlaght	Thomas Coote	1671

An indenture made on the second day of July in the year of our Lord one thousand six hundred and sixty seven in the twentyith year of the reign of our

soverign Lord Charles the second by the grace of God of Engalnd, Scotland, France and Ireland, King, defender of the faith BETWEEN Thomas Coote of Cootehill in the county of Cavan

Esquire of the one part and Patrick Laghy of Tawlaught in the county of Cavan Gentleman of the other part. WHEREAS the said Thomas Coote by deeds bearing date the day

before the Dah fordof xxx in consideration of ten shillings sterling of lawful money of England to him in hand payed <axon marketing forest> by the said Patrick Laghy HATH bargained and sold onto the said Patrick Laghy all the lands tennaments and testaments herinafter mentioned (that is to say) out of Tawlaught fifteen acres land wood profitable lands [flush and canteron]

measured out of Aughakilmore and twenty two acres of profitable land plantation measure out of Moydristan, sixty six acres --- woods, profitable lands plantation measure all which said lands and [Emissions] are lying and being in the Barony of Clonmahon and county of Cavan and ---- in the whole one hundred fifty acres xxx

profitable lands plantation measure amounting to two hundred forty six acres and wood English measure together with all [avsery] tho [heufor] Edifers buildings woods, underwoods

[slatters], boggs, mountains, hearths, Tenements [inhabitants] profit commodities advantages -- xx thereonto in any wise belonging ----- to HAVE AND hold

------ aforementioned [in said deed] --- for bargains and every ---- and every -----
aforementioned ------------------------------ commodities granted

before the date of [this deed] and --- forth July and --- YELDING and paying therefore onto the said Thomas Coote ---- aligns [friday the said Thomas the yearly]

rent of one [peppercorn] on the first day of November --- of the said year if the same be lawfully demanded ---- wherof the testotor of transferring ----

posession of the said Patrick Laghy and ---- possessed. xxx of all and every [Emmisses] with ---- HOW this Indenture [MnSosth] that the said Thomas Coote for an in xxx consideration of the just and full sum of three --- pounds Sterling lawfull money of England to him in hand at or before the [---lonig] or delivery thereof by the said Patrick Laghy

[duely] pays the next -------- of the said Thomas Coote doth hereby acknowledge and dother hereby ----- himself ---- fully satisfied and contented and payed and thereof an of every parte thereof doth acquite and discharged the said Patrick Laghy his heirs and aligns forever by [hold] x Gents HATH granted, reconfirmed ------- and for ever quit [Haymers] And by these Gents doth grant, reconfirm --- witness and forver quitt Claymed unto t he said Patrick Laghy his heirs and aligns the above mentioned -- of Tawlaught

[rent] fifteen
acres one rood profitable lands and plantation measured all with the lands and [Emissers]
are lying and being in the Barony of Clonmahon and county of Cavan and --
in the whole one hundred hundred fifty three acres of profitable land ------- plantation ----
amounting to two hundred and forty six acres [and wood] or [one rood] English ---- all
and every
[Laufer] Edificer, Tenements [Leridants] profitte, commodities advantages and app--
entances, tenants in any [wise] belonging to --- and also alll the estate, right, title, Interest
claym and demands which the said Thomas Coote his heirs and aligns hath or shall or
may [faud] at any tyme hereafter of into -- the [Emmises] and every or any part thereof
PROVIDED
Always that he the said Patrick Laghy his heirs and aligns shall RENDER or pay onto the
said Thomas Coote his heirs and aligns forever the yearly rent of two pounds and seven
shillings Sterling out of the aforesaid
[Emisee] it -- the said Thomas Coote his dwelling houses on the two --- days of payment
in the ----. That is to say of the [feast] of St Michael the [A-----] and the [A----tion]
Blessed virgin of St Mary by [awes] ans equal [postures] and if in ref any [prt] or [proll]
of aforesaid [reforward] rent shall happen to ------ or payed at any tyme that it shall --
lawfull to and for the said Thomas Coote his heirs and aligns to discharge xxx the
[Emisse] or any party thereof not only fopr the aforesaid Gent ---- but likewise of
[Stilling] [sford] by way of [nomine] pence out of each pound [wnt] [strnt] over and
above the ------ aforesaid four [avery] day the [wnk] shall have to be behind --- payed
after the days od payment and the [disk] of a [diftBop] found to [load] and that and take
away and dispose of according to law in [surfrefe] [prodaase] PROVIDED [aff---] th—
eres Laghy xxx his heirs and aligns shall from tyme to tyme and at tymes that suit at all
general [fff--fffines] and [safting] --- or to be --- in the county of Cavan
[free----] or ff ----- under the said Thomas Coote his heirs and aligns and likewise for
Patrick Laghy his heirs and aligns with ---- tenants shall and
hereby made lyable to [----forms] and fulfill all just duties [strife] and [servitors] the
court lessor court and Barons and manor courts of the said Thomas Coote his heirs and
aligns or [---after] at any tyme to be made or [---ted] as any other of the aforesaid tenants
holding from or under the said Thomas Coote his heirs or aligns shall may or sought to
or fulfill and be subject to all such matters ---- and ---- as the law requires in such ---- for
neglect of the same AND that the said Thomas Coote for himself his heirs ----
Diminishato and assigns doth hereby covenant promise grant and agree to and with the
said Patrick Laghy his heirs and aligns that the said Thomas Coote his heirs and align
shall
& will [sell?] warrant, defend uphold and maintain the [Emisses] herein before
mentioned or intended to be maintained and ----- part thereof with the Applentaces onto -
--
said Patrick Laghy his heirs and aligns forever against him the said Thomas Coote his
heirs and aligns and every of --- and allow every other person or persons whatsoever may
[moiny]
or [doinoring] or the they me or [derived?] any estate right, titles interest or demand of in
to or out of the [Emmisses] or any part thereof --- or any of them [exrect] of is alone
[ex--plas] thor visions made onto the said Thmoas Coote his heirs and aligns. An

WITNESSETH whereof the said parties to the said [grants] hand [h---wnts] interchangeably sell there lands and sealed the day and year first above written.

	From	To	Date
	Walter Ward	Patrick Laghy	1677

This Indenture made ther eleventh day of January in the year of our Lord God one thousand six hundred seventy seven and in the nine and twentieth year of the reign of our Sovereign Lord Charles the Second by the grace of God of England Scorland France and Ireland King defender of the faith Between Walter Ward of Drogheda in the county and towne of Drogheda aforesaid Gent of the one part and Patrick Laghy of Aghakilmore in the barony of Clonmahon within the county of Cavan aforesaid Gent of the other part. Witnesseth that the said Walter Ward for and in consideration of the full sum of fifty pounds sterling, the receipt whereof the said Walter Ward doth here ---- acknlowledged Hath bargained and sold and by there profits doth bargain and sell onto the said Patrick Laghy all the lands, tenants and ------ herein after mentioned that is to say out of Aghakilmore seventy acres profitable land plantation measure it lying and being in the Barony of Clonmahon within the county of Cavan together with and sinularly ----- houses and buildings woods, under woods, ways walks bogs, mountains --- tennaments ----- profits, commodities advantages and apprentices more unto in any way belong apportaining for ever without revocation and -- the said Walter Ward for him for life his heirs execs and aligns does covenant promise and grant to and with the said Patrick Laghy, his heirs execs and aligns that upon demand had on his land give and grant to and unto the ----- or assigns all deeds and convenences of and for the promise by the ---- in law of the said Patrick his --- be bought fit and lawfull and that at the ---- and strongest of said PAtrick , his heirs and assigns in witness thereof both parties have ----

----
Summary

Deed 11/1/1667

29th Year of Charles II Reign

Parties:

1. Walter Ward of Drogheda
2. Patrick Laghy of Aughakilmore

Patrick gave Walter Ward £50 for 70 Acres in Aughakilmore

	From	To	Date
	Thomas Lahy	(His Will)	1766

I leave to my wife – Margaret Lahy half part of the land and estate of which I am possessed of Upper Aghakilmore, likewise half my part and interest in Lavagh.

If she [wife] should marry again then the lands go to James Lahy my loving brother (and he has to pay wife £8 per year pension out of the lands)

If she [wife] doesn't marry then the lands (1/3) continue to her to the end of her natural life.

I bequeath to my daughter Jean [Jane ?] Lahy £50

There is now pending a lawsuit for the recovery from Mr Sam Taite of Curfade in county of Cavan and Execs of William Faith of said County deceased together with £50 which my said Executor to give and and pay upon a settlement made on him on his marriage bearing interest from the 3rd year after my decease and if the said Jane Lahy shall marry any person contrary to the consent of her mother or the consent of my Executor James then she only gets half of what is bequeathed to her. The other half goes to the children of Executor James Lahy.

I also bequeath to my wife three yellow cows usual about my house and all the best of my stock excepting my sheep and Baymore and Foal which I leave to my Executor James Lahy – I order to be sold and money paid out at interest for use and purpose of daughter Jean Lahy.

I leave and bequeath to my nephew Tobias Lahy son to my brother John Lahy deceased the sum of five pounds to be paid to him by my Executor James Lahy in the space of three years as he thinks fit. I also leave to my sister Mary Woods the sum of five pounds sterling to be paid in the space of three years as above. Also to Sarah McClean youngest daughter to James McClean of Ballachulan five pounds to be paid to be paid by my Executor provided she marries with the consent of her parents.

I also bequeath to my brother James Lahy all my sole right to the lands of Upper Aughakilmore, Lavagh, Aughafad, Mote, Aughakilmore Middle [Capragh] all lying and being in Ballymachugh- together with all arrears of rent due on any of them.

I also leave to my wife and daughter £10 out of the £20 14 Shillings which William Lahy of said Lavagh owes me, and the remainder to go to James (Executor).

I also order that what is due on a note I have of John Faith to be given to my wife and daughter.

I give to my daughter all my household furniture except a large oak table which I bequeath to my Executor James.

I likewise give my grey mare to my wife Margaret Lahy.

Witnesses:
John Johnson, William Lahy, Thomas Lye, John Faith

Analysis:

Thomas Owned lands in:
Lavagh
Upper Aughakilmore
Aughafad
Mote
Capragh

	Claimant	Against	Date
276 Prerogative Case Paper Salt Lake City – Family History Centre Film# 596411	Acheson	Margaret Lahy and James Lahy	3 March 1769

Citation on the part of Acheson against Lahy. Margaret Lahy and James Lahy the executors named in the last will of Thomas Lahy late of Aughakilmore in the county of Cavan, deceased – to appear before us – In the house of the Rt Hon Philip Tisdall Esq situate in Leinster, Dublin on 11 April next – To deposit in the registry of this court the said will and accept or refuse the brother of the executor thereof together with administration of all singles the goods etc of said deceased otherwise to his cause why letters of Adm of said deceased with the will amended should not be granted with Robert Acheson of the city of Dublin by financial seal of set deceased.

	Claimant	Against	Date
276 Prerogative Case Paper Salt Lake City – Family History Centre Film#	Acheson	Margaret Lahy and James Lahy	14 July 1769

596411			

Whereas there issued a citation against Margaret Lahy and James Lahy the executors named in the will of Thomas Lahy late of Aughakilmore Upper, Co Cavan, deceased. And whereas said citation was expected returned and whereas said Margaret Lahy and James Lahy the impungants in the above cited case have neglected to introduce said original will of said Thomas Lahy dead – Philip Tindall Esq Doctor of Laws – further proceeding in said business did at the petition of the proctor of said Robert Acheson decree a citation to issue against said Margaret Lahy and James Lahy in this case why they shall not be exonerated for their manifest contempt in not appearing.

Said Margaret and James Lahy to appear before us on 4th Nov next – there to show cause why should not be exonerated for their manifest contempt in not appearing at the time and place specified (and their effects) in said citation

	From	To	Date
[Wedding Articles]	Patrick Leahy	Eleanor Leahy	27/10/1846

Parties:
1. John Lahy of Aughakilmore
2. Patrick Lahy John's eldest son (also of Aughakilmore)
3. Patrick Lahy of Derrin
4. Eleanor Lahy - Daughter of Patrick of Derrin
5. Thomas Lahy of Drumeeny
6. John Strong of Kilnahard

John gives 40 acres of Land in Aughakilmore

Patrick (Derrin) gives £250 dowry
- £100 to be paid at solmization of the wedding
- £150 to be paid 5 years after
If Eleanor dies in that 5-year period, then the £150 doesn't have to be paid

Patrick (Junior) to pay £300 to Father John - in 5 years' time and 5 shillings at the wedding

John sold/rented land to Thomas Lahy and John Strong for 1 year for 5 shillings now in the possession of Patrick and Owen Sheridan [as payment for being trustees?]

John also gives half his farm to Patrick (Junior)

After the death of John then Thomas Lahy and John Strong to pay over the rents to Patrick (Junior)

In case Eleanor survives Patrick (Junior) then Thomas Lahy and John Strong to deliver the rents from the lands in possession of Pat and Owen Sheridan

If Patrick becomes insolvent or bankrupt then Thomas Lahy and John Strong to pay over the rent to Eleanor and she gets an annuity of £17 per year

If the payment of the annuity is late by 21 days or more then she and her assigns are entitled to enter the property and remove possessions to that value

If both Patrick and Eleanor die then Thomas Lahy and John Strong to ensure the rents are passed on to the children of the marriage.

If there are no male heirs (Of Patrick and Eleanor) then the land goes to the next surviving son of John Lahy (i.e. Patrick's oldest brother) - after £400 has been taken out of it to provide for Patrick and Eleanor's children.

Patrick (Junior) to give assistance and accommodation in his own house to his brothers and sisters should they need it.

Signed By

John Leahy
Harriet Leahy
Eleanor Leahy
Patt Leahy
Patrick Leahy
Thomas Leahy
Terence Smith

	From	To	Date
	John and Henry Lahy	Daniel Sheridan	23/4/1864

1. John and Henry Lahy of Aughakilmore
2 James and Daniel Sheridan of Ballina

John and Henry sold 4.5 acres to James and Daniel Sheridan for £46 8s

John and Henry still have to pay the taxes on it for 12 years

Signed:

Henry Lahey
John Lahey

James Sheridan
Daniel Sheridan

Witnessed:

John Brady
John Lahey

	From	To	Date
	John Lahy and Patrick Lahy	Thomas Sheridan Patrick Donoughue	1/5/1865

1. John Lahy and Patrick Lahy of Lower Aughakilmore
2. Thomas Sheridan of Lower Aughakilmore
3. Patrick Donoughue of Druminisilin

John and Patrick rent land in Aughakilmore (now in possession of Thomas Sheridan) for £20 per year for 3 years. Thomas Sheridan to become Patrick Donoughe's tenant

John and Patrick get £50 cash

	From	To	Date
	Patrick Leahy	William Leahy	6/8/1867

Parties:

1. Patrick Leahy
2 William Leahy

Lease of land now in William's possession - 10 Acres and one Rod including a meadow containing 3 roods.

Lease for 31 Years

Compensation for the sum of £150 devised to said William Leahy and charged upon the said lands under the last will and testament of John Leahy deceased father of the parties present

William to accept the £150 and therefore exonerate Patrick from making such payment

William to pay Patrick £10 10s rent annually for 31 years

If William doesn't pay his rent then Patrick's entitled to reclaim the £150

Notes:

Father John died in 1866
There's a son - William not listed anywhere else

Appendix A: Other Surnames Name Index

References

1. Leahy, David. The Cavan Leahys: Origins. 2016. Self-Published. ISBN-13: 978-0995663008 ISBN-10: 0995663009

2. Leahy, David. The Cavan Leahys: 1800-1950. Self-Published. ISBN-13: 978-0995663046

3. Lahey, Shirley. The Laheys: Pioneer settlers and sawmillers. Self-Published 2004. ISBN: 0646427644.

Deed Order Address

The Property Registration Authority
Registry of Deeds
Henrietta Street
Dublin 1

www.ingramcontent.com/pod-product-compliance
Lightning Source LLC
Chambersburg PA
CBHW081159270326
41930CB00014B/3216